SUPER FACTS
SCIENCE

Miles Kelly

Contents

Matter

Materials and chemicals

Energy, force and motion

Electricity, magnetism and radiation

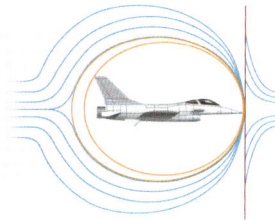

Frontiers of science

Technology

Atoms and molecules

⚙ Atoms are the tiny particles that make up every substance. An atom is the smallest basic building block of all ordinary matter.

⚙ Atoms are mostly empty space, but they contain even tinier particles known as subatomic particles.

⚙ Every atom has a dense core (nucleus) made up of two kinds of particle: protons and neutrons. Protons have a positive electrical charge, while neutrons have no charge. Even smaller, negatively charged particles – called electrons – whizz around the nucleus.

⚙ If an atom were the size of a sports arena, its nucleus would be roughly the size of a pea.

⚙ An atom is usually held together by the electromagnetic attraction between positively charged protons and negatively charged electrons, and by the 'strong nuclear force' that holds its nucleus together.

⚙ All the atoms that make up an element (a substance that cannot be broken down into any other substance) are identical. So, all the atoms inside a particular element have the same number of protons. The number of protons an atom has is known as its atomic number.

⚙ Typically, an atom has an equal number of protons and neutrons. An atom with an unequal balance of the two is called an isotope.

◄ *Inside this lithium atom, electrons (green) orbit a dense nucleus built up from protons (red) and neutrons (blue). There are three protons in the nucleus of a lithium atom, so its atomic number is three.*

⚙ Two billion atoms would fit on the full stop at the end of this sentence.

⚙ A molecule is two or more atoms that are bonded (held) together.

⚙ The atoms in a molecule are held together by chemical bonds (forces of attraction).

⚙ The structure (shape) of a molecule depends on the arrangement of chemical bonds that are holding its atoms together.

⚙ Molecules made from atoms of different elements are known as compounds. Most molecules like this are made of just two or three different types of atom.

⚙ If the atoms in the molecule of a compound were separated, the compound would cease to exist.

⚙ Chemical formulas indicate the make-up of a molecule or compound. For example, the formula for ammonia is NH_3. This tells you that an ammonia molecule consists of one nitrogen atom (N) and three hydrogen atoms (H).

⚙ 'Molecular mass' is the sum of the atomic weights of all the atoms making up a molecule.

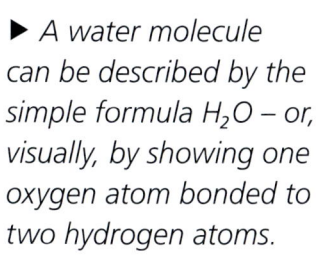

▶ *A water molecule can be described by the simple formula H_2O – or, visually, by showing one oxygen atom bonded to two hydrogen atoms.*

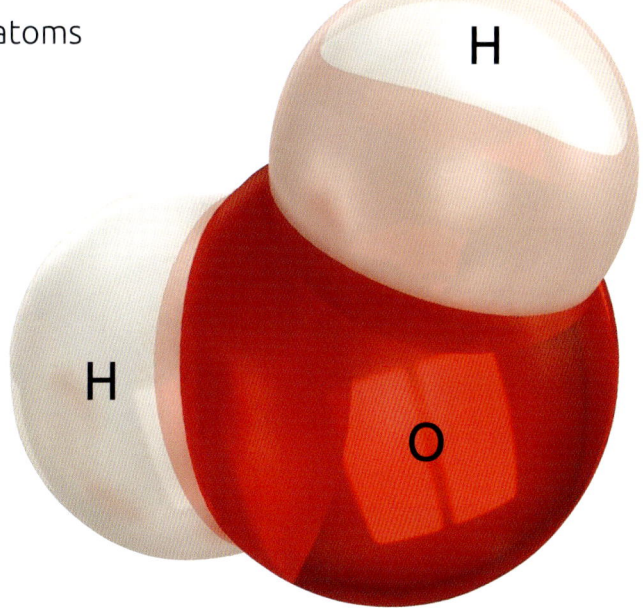

Electrons

⚙ Electrons are by far the smallest of the three main, 'stable' parts of every atom (the other two parts are the protons and neutrons). Normally, an atom has the same number of electrons as protons.

⚙ Electrons were discovered by English physicist J J Thomson in 1897. He studied the glowing rays made by electricity inside a glass tube (called a cathode ray tube) and realised that they were streams of tiny particles. Until then, an atom was thought to be a solid ball.

⚙ Electrons are much smaller and are more than 1,800 times lighter than protons. They contribute very little to an atom's mass.

⚙ Electrons are packets of energy travelling around the nuclei of atoms. It is impossible to pinpoint the exact location of an electron. Electrons do not orbit (circle) a nucleus as a planet circles the Sun. It is more accurate to think of them wrapping around the nucleus like a cloud.

▼ *Every type of atom has a different number of electrons. An atom's chemical character depends on the number of electrons in its outer shell. The electron shell structures of three common atoms are shown here.*

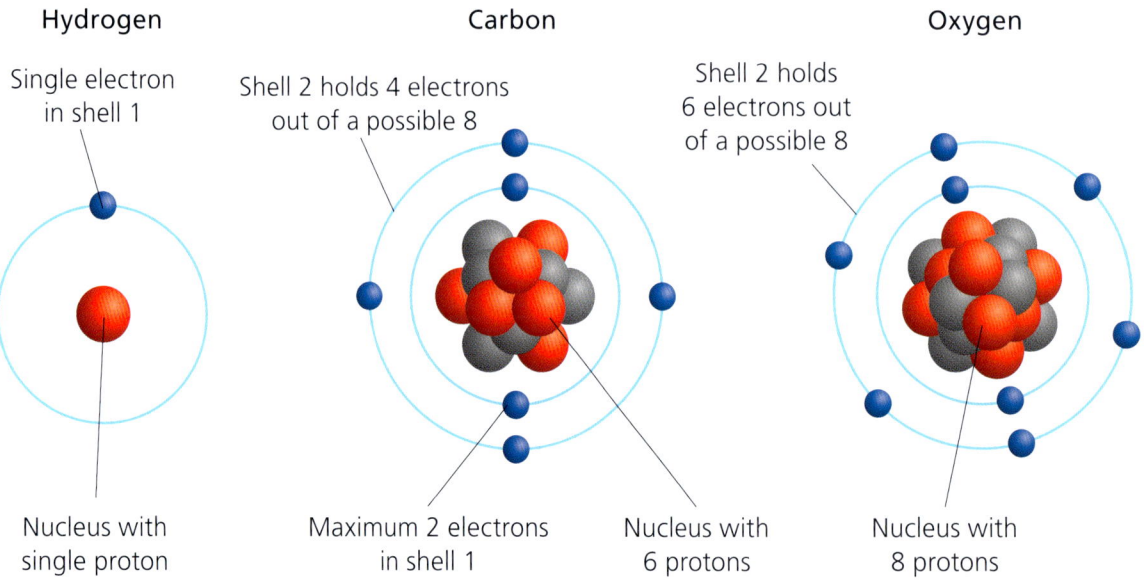

Hydrogen

Single electron in shell 1

Carbon

Shell 2 holds 4 electrons out of a possible 8

Oxygen

Shell 2 holds 6 electrons out of a possible 8

Nucleus with single proton

Maximum 2 electrons in shell 1

Nucleus with 6 protons

Nucleus with 8 protons

▲ *When iron atoms are exposed to water, including water vapour in the air, the oxygen atoms in the water attract electrons from the iron. This process, called an oxidation reaction, forms the flaky red compound iron oxide – also known as rust.*

⚙ Electrons have a tiny, negative electrical charge. This means they are attracted to positive electrical charges and repelled (pushed away) by other negative charges.

⚙ Electrons remain close to the nucleus because the protons in the nucleus have a combined positive charge that is equal to the strength of the electrons' combined negative charge.

⚙ Electrons circle the nucleus in layers. The distance between an electron and the nucleus depends on the energy level of the electrons in that layer. The greater an electron's energy, the farther it will be from the nucleus. In general, two electrons cannot occupy the same energy level. This is known as the exclusion principle.

⚙ Electrons are arranged in 'shells' at different distances around the nucleus. Each shell can hold a particular number of electrons: the first shell holds up to 2, the second up to 8, the third up to 18, the fourth up to 32, the fifth holds about 50 – and the sixth holds about 72.

Elements

⚙ Elements are the Universe's basic chemicals. Each element is made from atoms with a particular number of protons at its centre, or nucleus, which is indicated by the element's atomic number.

⚙ So far, 118 different elements have been recognised by scientists.

⚙ Chemists have organised the elements into groups on a chart known as the Periodic Table.

⚙ Among the most recently identified elements, at least 20 were created by scientists and do not exist in nature.

⚙ All of the most recently discovered elements have large, heavy atoms.

⚙ The lightest element is hydrogen. It has an atomic number of 1.

⚙ The densest element that occurs naturally is osmium, which has an atomic number of 76.

▶ *Iron (Fe) and other heavy elements were created when smaller atoms were fused together during giant supernova explosions in space.*

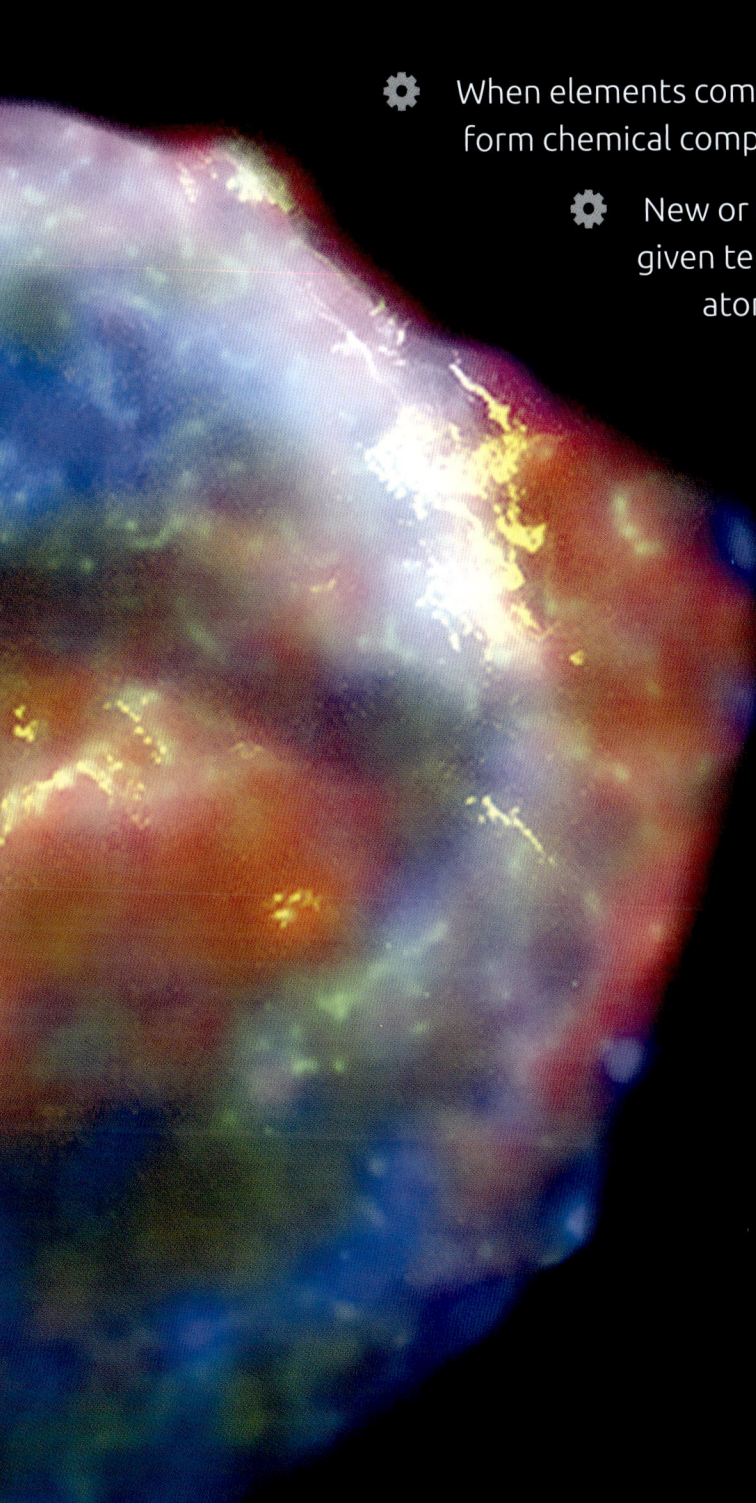

⚙ When elements combine with other elements, they form chemical compounds.

⚙ New or newly discovered elements are given temporary names based on their atomic number. For example, the element with the atomic number 116 was originally named ununhexium, because *un* is Latin for 'one' and *hex* is Latin for 'six'. It is now called livermorium.

⚙ American nuclear scientist Albert Ghiorso holds the record for the most elements discovered. Over the course of his career, he co-discovered twelve different elements.

DID YOU KNOW?
Scientists fired calcium atoms at californium atoms to create the element oganesson, which has an atomic number of 118 and the heaviest-known atoms.

Compounds and bonds

⚙ Atoms link together to create molecules by forming chemical bonds.

⚙ Atoms are able to form a chemical bond when they are 'missing' electrons. Oxygen has only six electrons in its outer shell, meaning it can easily form bonds with another atom that will share or 'donate' those 'missing' two electrons.

⚙ Compounds are substances that are made when the atoms of two or more different elements join together.

⚙ The properties of a compound are usually very different from the properties of the elements from which the compound is made.

⚙ A compound's scientific name is usually a combination of the names of the elements it is composed of. It might have a different 'common' name, however: sodium chloride is more commonly known as 'salt'.

⚙ All molecules in a compound have identical combinations of atoms.

⚙ Ionic bonds occur when non-metal, 'electron-hungry' atoms gain electrons from 'electron-rich' metal atoms. The metal atom readily donates electrons to become a positively charged ion, while the non-metal atom gladly receives electrons to become a negatively charged ion – with a more stable outer shell (see below).

▶ The transfer of electrons (from the sodium atoms to the chlorine atoms) creates oppositely charged 'ions' that are then attracted to each other, forming the ionic bond.

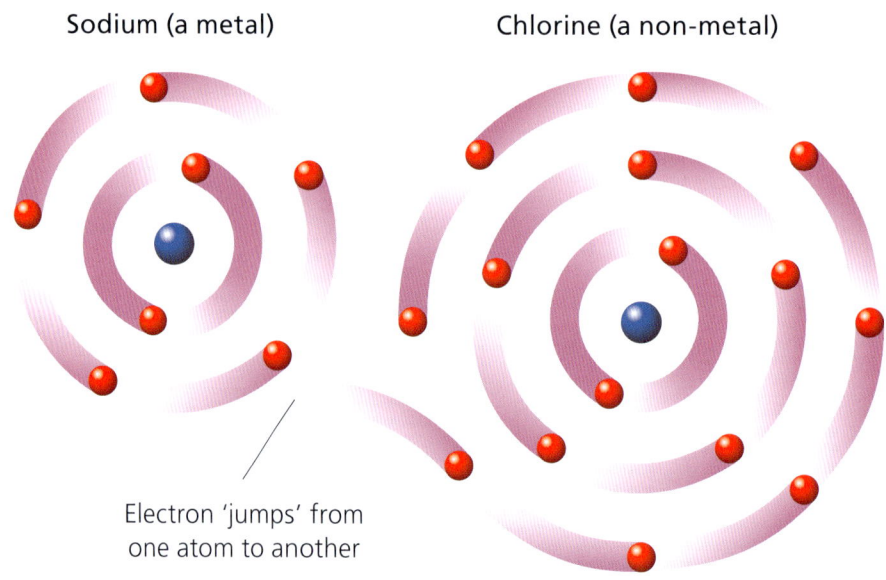

Sodium (a metal)

Chlorine (a non-metal)

Electron 'jumps' from one atom to another

▼ *Water is a common compound. It is formed through covalent bonds – one oxygen atom shares electrons with two hydrogen atoms.*

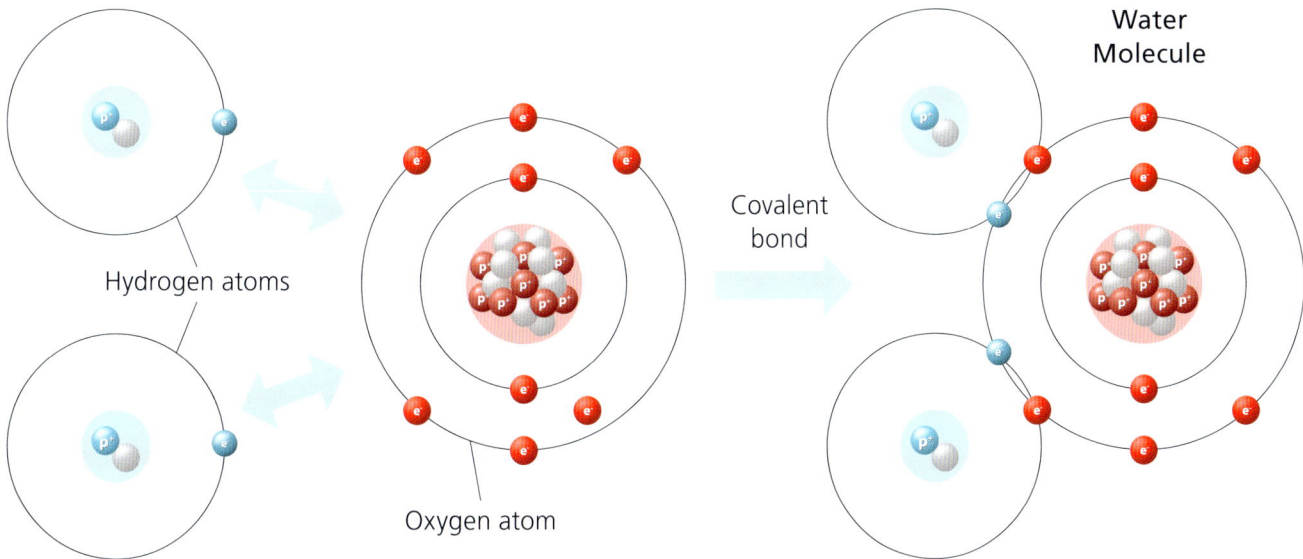

Hydrogen atoms

Oxygen atom

Covalent bond

Water Molecule

⚙ Sodium chloride (see page 12), or NaCl, consists of sodium ions (Na⁺) and chloride ions (Cl⁻). This compound (otherwise known as table salt) is held together by ionic bonds, or the 'electrostatic' attraction between oppositely charged ions – the positively charged sodium ions and the negatively charged chloride ions.

⚙ Covalent bonds occur when atoms share electrons. The shared electrons are negatively charged, so they are all equally drawn to the positive nuclei of both atoms. The atoms are held together by the attraction between each nucleus and the shared electrons. This type of sharing allows each atom to complete its outer electron shell, which makes the atoms more stable.

⚙ A chemical formula tells you which and how many atoms a molecule contains. The chemical formula for water is H_2O, because every water molecule has two hydrogen (H) atoms and one oxygen (O) atom.

⚙ There are around 118 known chemical elements – and they combine in countless ways to form many millions of different compounds.

Chemical reactions

⚙ A chemical reaction occurs when two or more elements or compounds interact chemically, breaking old bonds between atoms and making new ones.

⚙ The chemicals in a chemical reaction are called the reactants. The results are known as the products.

⚙ The products of a chemical reaction contain the same atoms as the reactants – but in different combinations.

⚙ The products of a reaction will have the same total mass as the reactants, but their masses may be harder to quantify if they have been converted into different states of matter during the reaction.

⚙ Most reactions cannot be reversed, which means the products cannot be changed back into the reactants. For example, toasting bread causes an 'irreversible' chemical reaction.

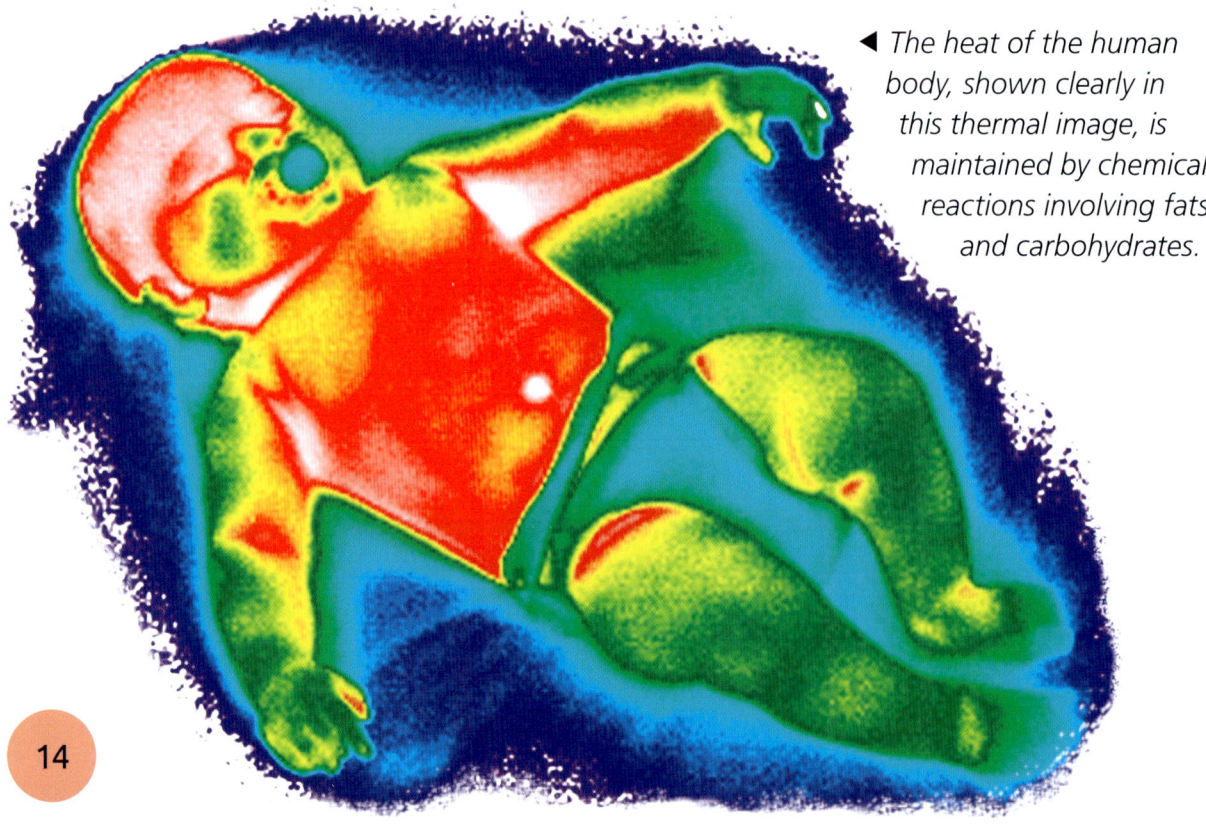

◄ The heat of the human body, shown clearly in this thermal image, is maintained by chemical reactions involving fats and carbohydrates.

▲ *When potassium iodide is added to a mixture of hydrogen peroxide and liquid soap, the iodide acts as a catalyst, causing the hydrogen peroxide to decompose rapidly. This 'exothermic' reaction produces water, oxygen and heat. The reaction traps the oxygen inside the soap, creating foam – which can get very hot!*

⚙ In a chemical reaction, elements may join to form compounds, while the elements making up compounds may be separated – or find new partners in other compounds.

⚙ A catalyst is a substance that speeds up a chemical reaction or enables a chemical reaction to take place.

⚙ Nearly all reactions involve energy. Some involve light or electricity, but most involve heat. Reactions that give out heat are known as exothermic. Those that draw in heat are called endothermic.

⚙ Oxidation is a reaction in which oxygen combines with another substance. Burning is a form of oxidation: as a material (the fuel) burns, it combines with oxygen in the air. Reduction is a reaction in which a substance loses oxygen.

⚙ There are five basic types of chemical reaction: combustion, synthesis (or combination), decomposition, single replacement (or single displacement) and double replacement (or double displacement).

Solutions

⚙ A solution is a liquid that has another substance 'dissolved' within it.

⚙ The liquid in a solution is called the solvent. The solid dissolved in a solution is the solute.

⚙ When a solid dissolves, its molecules separate and mix completely with the liquid.

⚙ As a solute dissolves, the solution becomes more concentrated until at last it is 'saturated'. This means that no more solute will dissolve.

⚙ If a saturated solution is heated, the solvent molecules gain more energy and move around faster. This creates more space in between the molecules, which enables more of the solute to dissolve.

⚙ If a saturated solution cools or is left to evaporate (the process in which a liquid turns to vapour) there will be less room for the solute. This causes the solute to precipitate (come out of the solution).

⚙ Precipitated solute molecules often link together to form crystals.

▶ *A cup of tea is made up of the solvent (water) and a number of solutes: the tea, milk and perhaps sugar. The process of combining the solutes and the solvent can be accelerated by stirring the liquid mixture.*

Mixtures

⚙ Mixtures are substances that contain two or more different ingredients (elements or compounds). They can be gases, liquids or solids. Many common substances are mixtures, including milk, oil and the air we breathe (a mix of oxygen, nitrogen and other gases).

⚙ The properties of a mixture are often a combination of the properties of its ingredients. For example, a mixture of sugar and water is both sweet-tasting and wet.

⚙ Mixtures can often be separated into their ingredients using physical processes. For example, you can use a sieve to separate solids with smaller particles from those that have larger particles.

⚙ The process of distillation works by separating liquids (in a mixture) that evaporate (turn to vapour) and condense (turn to liquid) at different temperatures. The mixture is heated to a certain temperature to evaporate a specific liquid. Droplets of the separated vapour are collected as it cools and condenses.

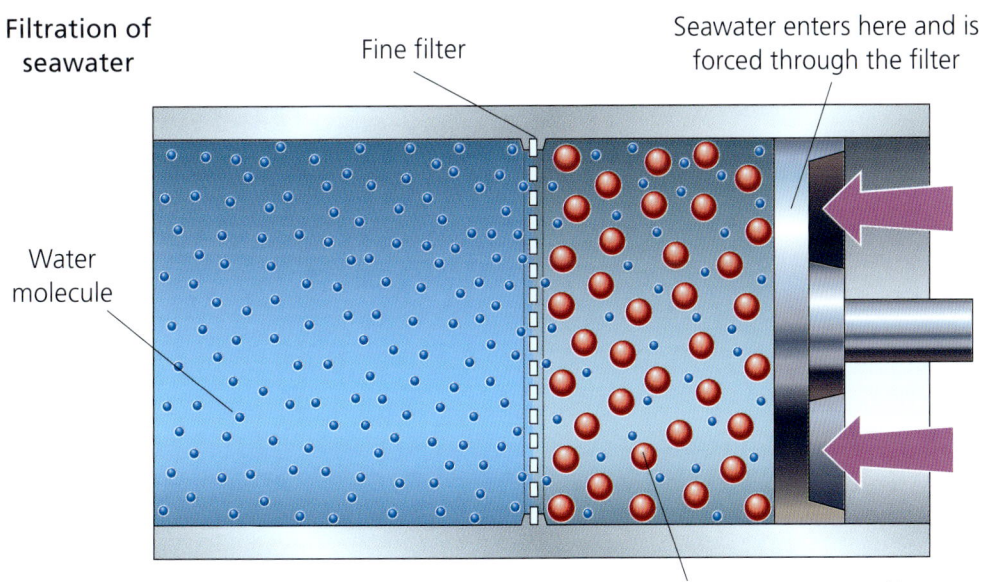

Filtration of seawater

Fine filter

Seawater enters here and is forced through the filter

Water molecule

Salt molecules cannot pass through the filter

▲ *The salt is removed from seawater by pushing it through a very fine filter, making it drinkable. This process is called reverse osmosis.*

17

Acids and alkalis

⚙ Acids are solutions that are made when certain substances containing hydrogen dissolve in water.

⚙ Hydrogen atoms have a single electron. When acid-making substances dissolve in water, the hydrogen atoms lose their electron, becoming positively charged ions (see page 12: an ion is an atom that has either gained or lost electrons).

⚙ The strength of an acid depends on how many hydrogen ions form. Mild acids, such as acetic or ethanoic acid (found in vinegar), have a sharp or sour taste. Strong acids, such as hydrochloric acid, are highly corrosive (they can dissolve metals).

⚙ A base is the opposite of an acid. Weak bases, such as baking powder, taste bitter and feel soapy. Strong bases such as bleach are corrosive.

⚙ A base that dissolves in water is called an alkali. Alkalis contain negatively charged ions – typically, ions of hydrogen and oxygen, known as hydroxide ions.

⚙ When you add an acid to an alkali, in the correct proportions, both substances are neutralised (they cancel each other out). The acid and alkali react with each other to form water and a salt.

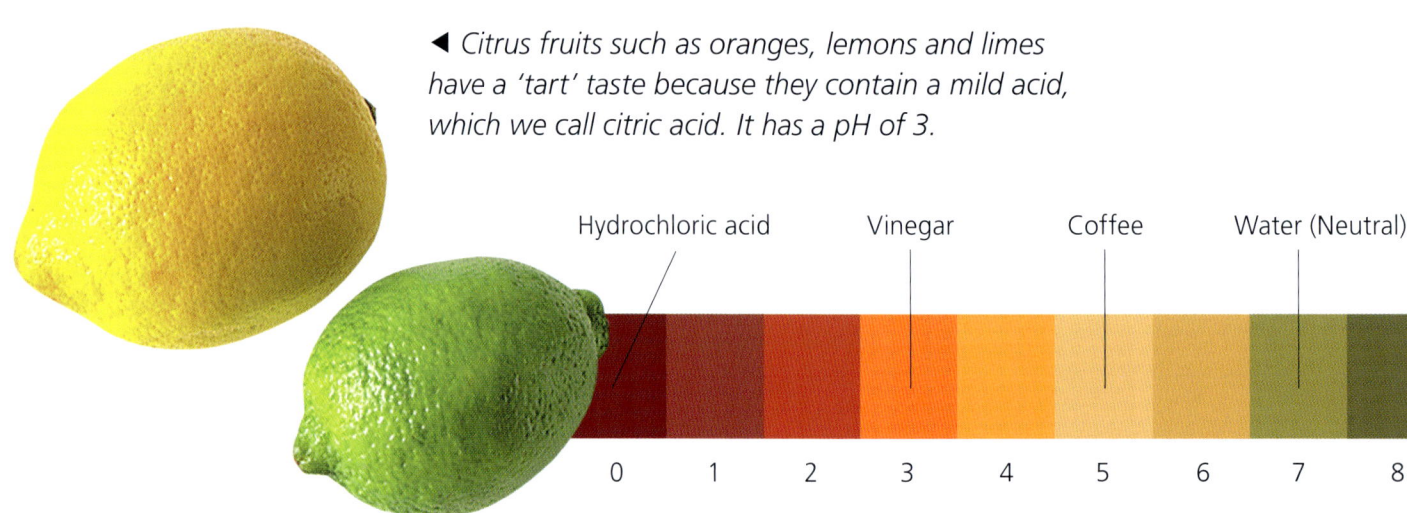

◀ *Citrus fruits such as oranges, lemons and limes have a 'tart' taste because they contain a mild acid, which we call citric acid. It has a pH of 3.*

Hydrochloric acid   Vinegar   Coffee   Water (Neutral)

0   1   2   3   4   5   6   7   8

DID YOU KNOW?
Hydrochloric acid in the stomach is essential for digestion. It has a pH of between 1 and 2.

⚙ The strength of an acid can be measured on the pH scale. The strongest acid has a pH of 0. The strongest alkali has a pH of 14. Pure water has a pH of about 7. It is neutral – neither acid nor alkali.

⚙ Chemists use 'indicators' to test for acidity. An indicator is a substance, such as the solution on litmus paper, which changes colour depending on the pH of the solution it contacts.

⚙ There are acids that are so strong they cannot be measured on the pH scale. These acids are called superacids.

⚙ Fluoroantimonic acid is a superacid that is billions of times stronger than 100 per cent sulphuric acid. It is so strong that it can corrode rocks, ceramics and glass. It has to be stored in special Teflon-lined containers.

▶ *Household cleaners often contain alkalis to help them break down slimy grease and fat. Some cleaners have a pH of 10.*

▼ *Universal indicator on the pH scale reveals acidity or alkalinity.*

Baking powder   Bleach

9   10   11   12   13   14

LEMON
KITCHEN
DISSOLVES G
ILLS BACT

WASHING-UP
LIQUID

Soaps and salts

⚙ Soaps and detergents are salts that can remove grease and dirt. They are known as surfactants, or surface-acting agents. Soaps are natural, while detergents are synthetic (human-made).

⚙ Surfactants are emulsifiers: they can break down the 'surface tension' of two molecules that normally repel each other, allowing them to mix. This enables water to mix with dirt and oil and wash it all away.

⚙ Surfactant molecules are composed of two parts: one part is hydrophilic (attracted to water), while the other is hydrophobic (repelled by water).

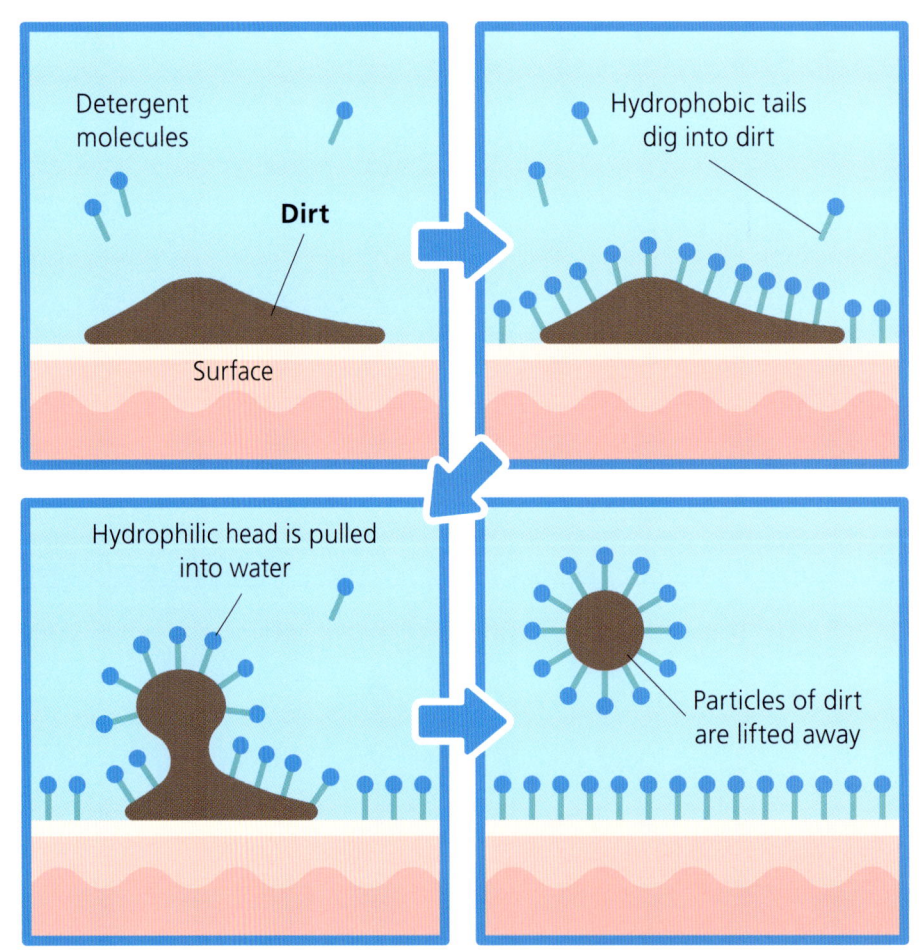

▲ *The hydrophobic tail of the soap molecule digs into dirt and grease, allowing it to be easily lifted away into the water by the hydrophilic head.*

▲ *Soap nuts are berries of the soapberry tree. They contain a natural, soapy chemical that can be used to wash clothes and other textiles.*

⚙ The hydrophobic tail of a surfactant molecule digs its way into the dirt (see page 20), while the hydrophilic head is drawn to the water.

⚙ Surfactants increase water's ability to make things wet by reducing the water's surface tension.

⚙ Soap is made from natural substances including fats or oil combined with alkalis (such as sodium or potassium hydroxide). Most also include perfumes, colours and germicides (germ-killers) as well as a surfactant.

⚙ Enzymes are molecules that speed up chemical reactions. Certain enzymes can be added to detergents to help break down stains from natural substances such as blood, grease and starch.

⚙ Biosurfactants are natural surfactants. Organisms such as bacteria, yeasts and fungi produce biosurfactants that are environmentally-friendly tools for cleaning up oil spillages.

States of matter

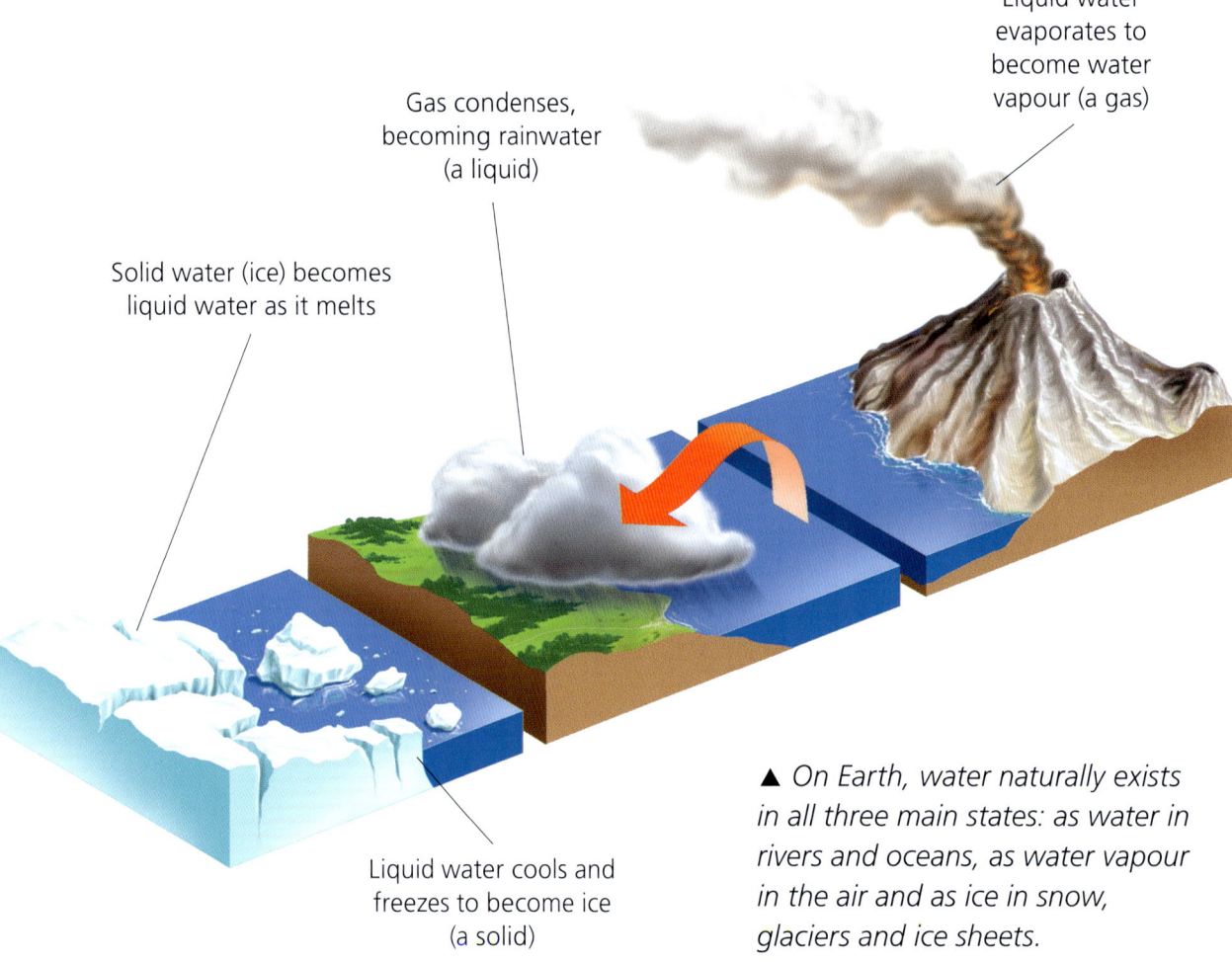

Liquid water evaporates to become water vapour (a gas)

Gas condenses, becoming rainwater (a liquid)

Solid water (ice) becomes liquid water as it melts

Liquid water cools and freezes to become ice (a solid)

▲ *On Earth, water naturally exists in all three main states: as water in rivers and oceans, as water vapour in the air and as ice in snow, glaciers and ice sheets.*

⚙ Most substances can exist in three states – solid, liquid and gas. These are known as the three fundamental states of matter. As temperature and pressure change, a substance's state of matter will change.

⚙ The fourth fundamental state of matter is plasma, which is a type of gas in which the particles are electrically charged. This process is called ionisation, and it occurs naturally in lightning and auroras.

⚙ As temperatures rise, solids melt to become liquids. As they rise further, liquids evaporate to become vapours or gases. The temperature at which a solid melts is known as its melting point.

- The boiling point is the maximum temperature a liquid can reach before it fully turns to gas, although liquids can partially evaporate at well below their boiling point.

- When a gas cools, its molecules slow down until bonds form between them to create drops of liquid – a process we call condensation.

- There are multiple man-made states of matter. Bose-Einstein condensates were first created in 1995. They form when temperatures are so low that all atoms almost stop moving completely.

- In 1827, Scottish botanist Robert Brown examined microscopic pollen grains in water and saw that they were being knocked about by moving molecules too small to be seen. This is known as Brownian motion.

- The 'kinetic' theory of matter explains the changes from solid to liquid to gas in terms of the movement of these molecules.

- Solids have a definite shape because their molecules are bonded into a rigid structure. Their particles vibrate, rather than move freely.

- A liquid flows and takes the shape of any container into which it is poured. Its particles are bonded loosely enough for them to move over and around each other.

- A gas, such as air, does not have any definite shape or fixed volume, because its molecules are barely bound together at all – they are free to move around in all directions.

▶ In a plasma globe, electricity turns gases into a glowing, charged plasma filled with beams of light that move when a hand touches the globe's surface.

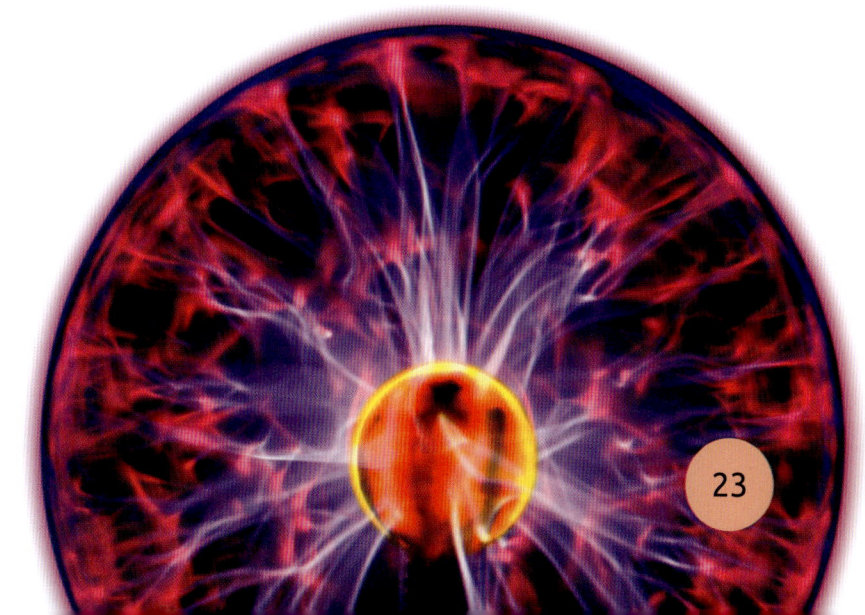

Crystals

⚙ Crystals are particular kinds of solid that are made from a regular arrangement, or lattice, of atoms. Most rocks and metals are crystals, as are snowflakes and most salts.

⚙ Most crystals have regular, geometrical shapes with smooth faces and sharp corners. They grow in dense masses, such as metals. Some crystals grow separately, like grains of sugar.

⚙ Crystals were named after chunks of quartz that the ancient Greeks called *krystallos*, which they believed were unmeltable ice.

⚙ Crystallization is the process by which crystals form. It occurs when liquid evaporates or molten solids cool, causing the chemicals dissolved in them to solidify.

⚙ Crystals grow as individual atoms or molecules attach themselves to the lattice, just as icicles form when water freezes onto them.

⚙ The smallest crystals are microscopic – but, occasionally, crystals of a mineral (such as beryl) may grow to the size of telegraph poles.

⚙ A liquid crystal is a crystal that can flow, like a liquid, but has a regular pattern of atoms, like a solid.

⚙ A liquid crystal may change colour or go dark when the alignment of its atoms is disrupted by electricity or heat. Liquid crystal displays (LCDs) – such as those used in TV screens – use a tiny electric current to make the crystals 'twist' the light passing through them.

⚙ X-ray crystallography uses X-rays to study the structure of atoms in crystals. It is also used to study biological molecules, and it is how we identified the structure of many important life substances – such as DNA.

⚙ Gemstones are a type of crystal made of mineral deposits. Gemstones are considered to be valuable because of their interesting colours or reflective effects. They are often polished and used to create decorative jewellery or other small items.

◄ *Crystals often form from mineral-rich liquids found on the lining of cavities in hollow rocks (called geodes).*

The Periodic Table

⚙ There are 118 known elements. Of these, 92 are known to occur naturally on Earth, while the rest were created by scientists. Two of these, plutonium and neptunium, are now known to occur naturally.

⚙ In the table, all the elements are ordered by atomic number (the number of protons in an atom of a particular element). The atomic number is shown at the top-left corner of every element entry.

⚙ The atomic mass is shown at the bottom left of every entry. If you subtract an element's atomic number from its mass, the result (rounded to the nearest whole number) is a guide to how many neutrons there are in that element's atoms. For example, calcium's atomic number is 20 and its mass is 40, so it has 20 neutrons.

⚙ The vertical columns in the table are called groups. The horizontal rows are called periods. As you move across the table, from left to right, the number of electrons increases.

⚙ Each group contains elements with a certain number of electrons in their outer shell. This is what largely determines each element's 'character'. All the elements in each group have similar properties.

⚙ Each period starts (on the left) with a highly reactive alkali metal of Group 1. Each atom of the elements in Group 1 has a single electron in its outer shell. Every period ends (on the right) with a stable 'noble' gas of Group 18. These elements have the full number of electrons in their outer shell – and so they are unreactive.

⚙ Russian chemist Dmitri Mendeleev published a periodic table in 1869, which paved the way for today's version. Mendeleev's table had only 63 elements on it – but he was able to use it to predict the existence of elements that had not yet been discovered, such as gallium.

▶ *The Periodic Table (right) arranges all the chemical elements in columns and rows according to their atomic number. This helps to indicate any similarities between them in terms of their chemical properties.*

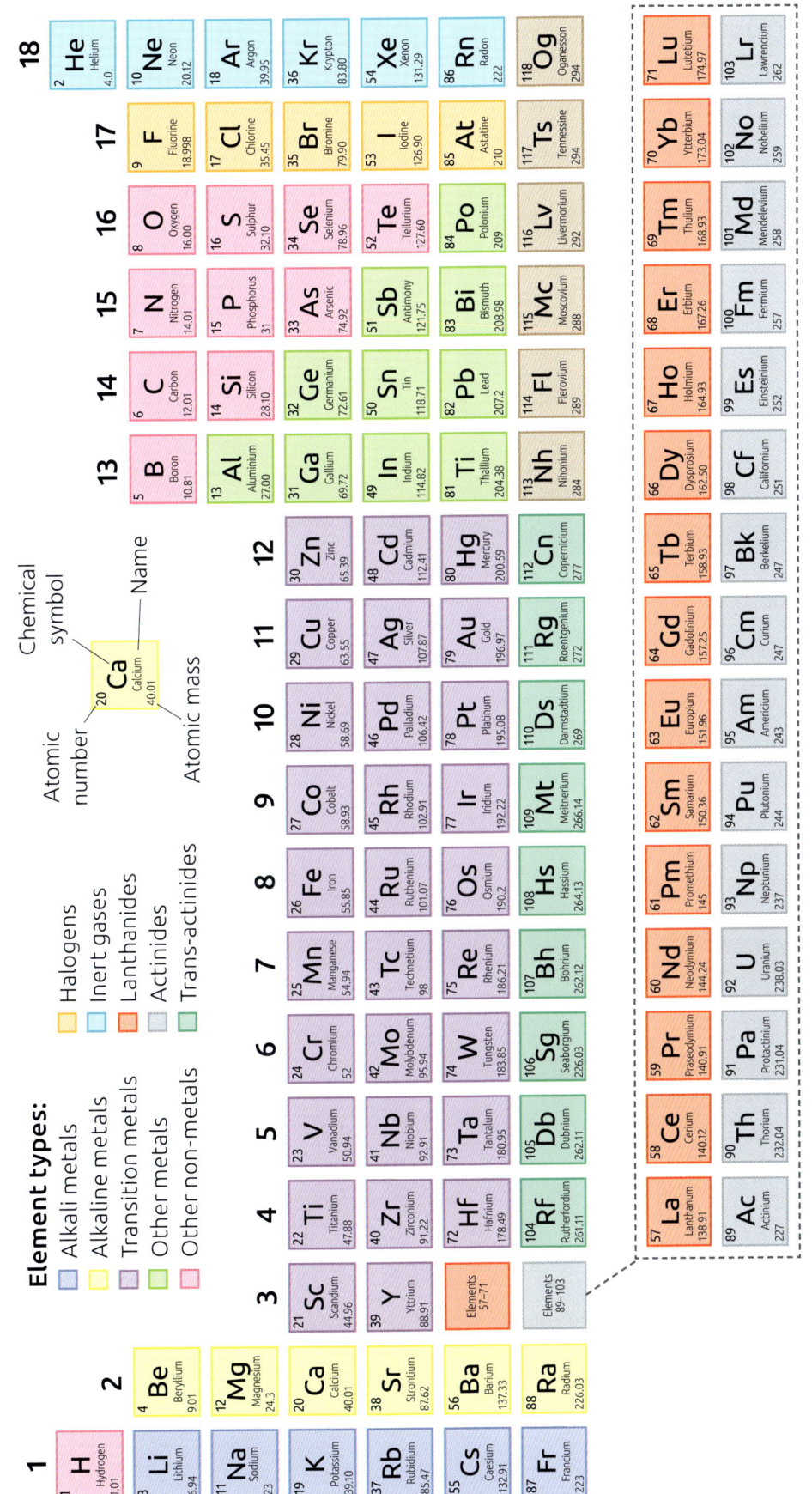

Element types:

- Alkali metals
- Alkaline metals
- Transition metals
- Other metals
- Other non-metals
- Halogens
- Inert gases
- Lanthanides
- Actinides
- Trans-actinides

Chemical symbol — Name

Atomic number — Atomic mass

| 20 Ca Calcium 40.01 |

Metals and alloys

▲ *Molten gold is poured into a graphite cast (mould) at a smelting plant. When the precious metal cools, it forms bars that are approximately 99.99 per cent pure.*

⚙ Approximately 75 per cent of all the known elements are metals.

⚙ Metals are typically hard but malleable, which means they can be hammered into thin sheets or pressed into shape without breaking.

⚙ Metals are usually shiny, strong, and tend to conduct (transmit) heat and electricity well.

⚙ Instead of forming separate molecules, metal atoms are 'knitted' together in criss-cross 'lattice' structures by their metallic bonds.

⚙ All metals have electron shells that are less than half full. In chemical reactions, metals give up their electrons to non-metals (see pages 12–13).

⚙ Most metals occur naturally in the ground within rocks known as ores.

⚙ Mercury is the only metal that is liquid at normal temperatures. It melts at a chilly –38.9°C.

DID YOU KNOW?
Tungsten has the highest melting point of any metal. It melts at around 3,422°C.

⚙ An alloy is a human-made mixture of at least one metal – combined with other metals or non-metals – created by melting the elements together and then allowing them to cool and solidify. This process can create alloys with properties for particular uses, such as enhanced strength, hardness or resistance to corrosion (breaking down).

⚙ Bronze is an alloy of copper and tin. Copper is a soft metal, so combining it with tin makes it stronger. People discovered how to create bronze more than 5,000 years ago.

⚙ Steel is a strong alloy composed of iron and traces of carbon and other metals, such as tungsten. It is used in a variety of modern products, from engineering materials to kitchen equipment.

⚙ Spacecraft are normally made from incredibly light, tough alloys such as aluminium and lithium.

⚙ Titanium alloys are among the strongest, lightest and most heat- and corrosion-resistant of all the elements. This is why they are commonly used in the construction of aircraft and space vehicles.

▼ *Jet engines need to be incredibly tough – but also incredibly light. Luckily, titanium alloys have these useful properties.*

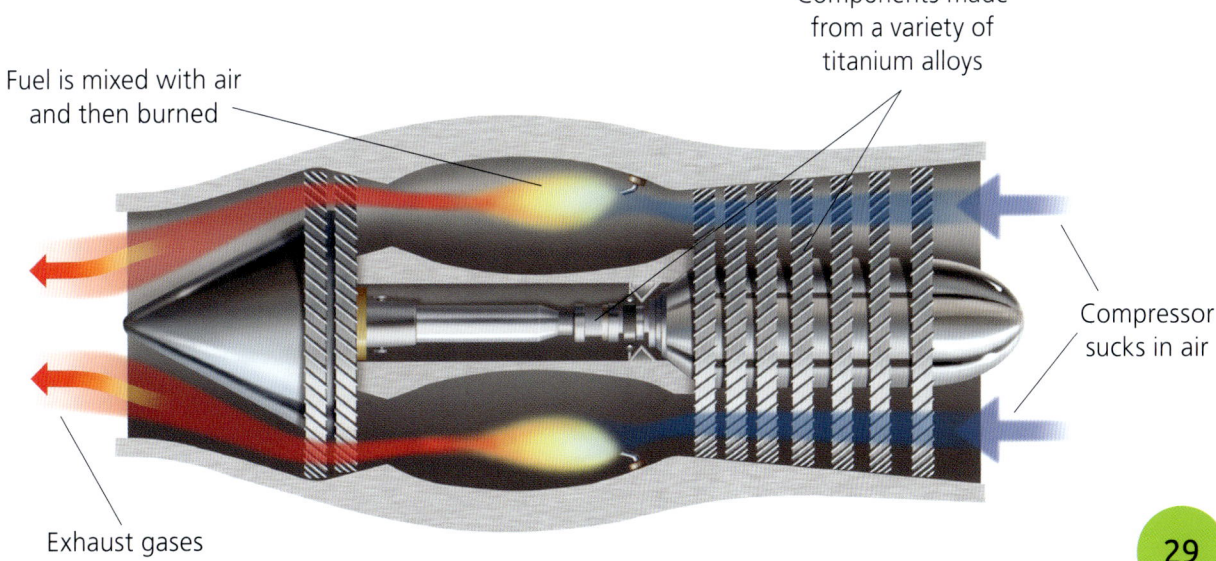

Components made from a variety of titanium alloys

Fuel is mixed with air and then burned

Compressor sucks in air

Exhaust gases

Aluminium

◄ *The primary ore of aluminium, called bauxite, forms deep, powdery layers in the ground. It is found in tropical and subtropical parts of the world. This photograph shows eroded bauxite rock, exposed above ground.*

⚙ Aluminium (Al) is by far the most common metal on Earth's surface, making up approximately 8 per cent of the planet's crust.

⚙ Aluminium never occurs naturally in its pure form – it is typically found combined with other chemical elements within minerals, rocks and clays. It is extracted from its main ore, bauxite.

⚙ Layers of the soft ore rock bauxite – mostly composed of aluminium hydroxide minerals – provide our main source of aluminium.

⚙ Alum powders, made from aluminium compounds, are used in the process of dyeing fabric.

⚙ In 1808, English Scientist Humphry Davy established the existence of aluminium. Danish scientist Hans Ørsted was the first to isolate a small quantity of the metal, in its pure form, in 1825.

⚙ Aluminium is silver in colour when freshly refined, but it quickly tarnishes (loses its sheen) and turns white when exposed to the air.

⚙ This element is very slow to corrode (break down) and is one of the lightest metals, with lithium (Li) being the lightest of all.

⚙ Aluminium oxide can crystallize into one of the hardest minerals, corundum, which is used to sharpen knives.

⚙ Aluminium melts at about 660°C and boils at around 2,467°C.

⚙ Guinea, Australia and China are the world's largest producers of bauxite.

⚙ Each year, tens of millions of tonnes of aluminium are made globally.

⚙ China produces approximately 60 per cent of the world's aluminium.

⚙ Lots of products and machines are made from aluminium, because it is lightweight and resistant to corrosion.

▲ *Duraluminium is a high-strength alloy composed of aluminium and a little copper and manganese. It is tough, durable and lightweight, making it ideal for the manufacture of aircraft.*

Iron and steel

⚙ Iron is the most common element, making up around 35 per cent of the Earth. Most of it is located within the planet's core.

⚙ Iron is found in iron ores, rather than in its pure form. The ores are heated in blast furnaces to extract molten (liquefied) iron.

▼ *Molten (liquefied) iron is poured into a steelmaking furnace inside a steel mill. The temperature of the liquid metal is approximately 1,538°C.*

- The chemical symbol for iron is Fe – from the word *ferrum*, which is Latin for 'iron'. Iron compounds are described as ferrous or ferric.

- Iron conducts heat and electricity well and dissolves in water very slowly. Iron is easily magnetized, but also loses its magnetism easily.

- Iron oxide (rust) forms when iron combines with oxygen, especially in the presence of moisture. Iron oxide has a red, flaky appearance.

- Cast iron is iron that contains 2–4 per cent carbon and 1–3 per cent silicon. It is suitable for pouring into casts, or moulds. Removing carbon from iron creates wrought iron, which is almost pure. Wrought iron is easier to bend and shape into railings and gates.

- Iron is made into steel by adding traces of carbon. Steel has many industrial uses, such as in cars, railway lines, bridges and buildings.

- A steel cooker, kettle or kitchen sink is made 'stainless' by adding chromium, which keeps the steel permanently shiny and smooth.

- Sixty per cent of all steel is made by the Basic Oxygen Process, in which oxygen is blasted over molten iron to burn out impurities.

- Special alloy steels – such as chromium steels – can be made from scrap iron (which is low in impurities) in an electric arc furnace.

- The human body contains around 3–4 g of iron. Iron is essential for the production of haemoglobin, a special protein in your red blood cells that binds to oxygen and carries it through your bloodstream.

DID YOU KNOW?
Mars is known as the Red Planet because of the high levels of iron oxide in its soil.

Copper

⚙ Copper has been used for more than 10,000 years. It was one of the first metals to be used by humans.

⚙ It is one of the few metals that occurs naturally in its pure form. However, most of the copper we use today comes from ores such as cuprite.

⚙ The largest deposits of pure copper are found in volcanic lavas in the Andes Mountains, Chile.

⚙ Copper is by far the best and most cost-efficient conductor of electricity, so it is widely used in electrical cables.

⚙ It is also an excellent conductor of heat, which is why it is used to make the bases of saucepans.

⚙ Copper is so ductile (easily stretched) that a copper rod as thick as a finger can be stretched out thinner than a human hair.

⚙ After being exposed to the air for some time, copper gets a green coating of copper carbonate. This is called verdigris, which means 'green' in Greek.

⚙ Verdigris was historically used as a pigment in painting, but exposure to it can cause heavy metal poisoning in humans. Safer alternatives are now used.

DID YOU KNOW?
Copper is vital to your health. Traces of it help to carry oxygen around your body, maintain hair colour and make hormones.

◄ *The familiar pale green colour of the Statue of Liberty in New York City, USA, comes from a thin coating of copper carbonate that has formed throughout its surface.*

Calcium

⚙ Calcium is a soft, silvery-white metal. It does not occur naturally in its pure form, but is the fifth most abundant element on Earth.

⚙ Most calcium compounds are white solids called limes. These include substances such as chalk, enamel and limescale.

⚙ Limelight was the bright light used by theatres in the days before electricity, made by applying a mix of oxygen and hydrogen to pellets of calcium.

⚙ Quicklime is calcium oxide, so-called because, when water drips on it, it twists and swells as if it is alive ('quick' is an old word for 'living').

⚙ Slaked lime is calcium hydroxide. It may be called 'slaked' because it slakes (quenches) a plant's thirst for lime in acid soils.

⚙ Calcium adds rigidity to bones and teeth and helps to control muscles. Your body cannot make calcium itself, so it gets it from your diet – from sources such as milk, soya, beans and almonds.

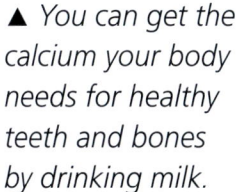

▲ *You can get the calcium your body needs for healthy teeth and bones by drinking milk.*

◀ *The eggshell that protects a chick, until it is ready to hatch, is usually made from calcium carbonate.*

Oxygen

⚙ Oxygen is the second most plentiful element on Earth. It is a colourless, odourless, tasteless gas, which makes up about 21 per cent of the air. It is one of the most reactive elements, so it is usually found in compounds with other chemicals.

⚙ Molecules of oxygen in the air are made from two oxygen atoms. Molecules of the gas ozone have three oxygen atoms.

⚙ Oxygen becomes liquid at –182.962°C and freezes at –218.4°C.

⚙ Living organisms are dependent upon oxygen because it joins up with other chemicals in living cells, such as glucose, to create energy. This process is known as cellular respiration.

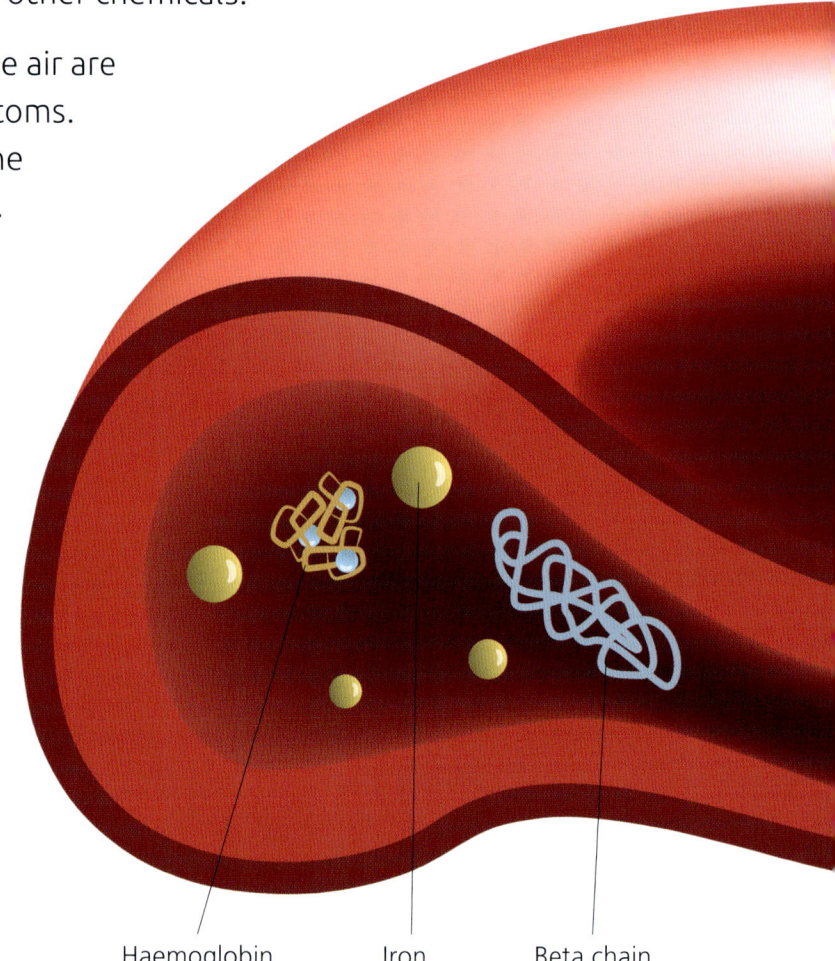

Haemoglobin   Iron   Beta chain

DID YOU KNOW?
Most of the oxygen in the air is produced by marine organisms called algae.

▲ All healthy red blood cell contain haemoglobin, the protein that binds to oxygen molecules (O_2).

⚙ Liquid oxygen (LOX) is combined with fuels such as kerosene to produce rocket fuel.

⚙ During the 1770s, oxygen was discovered by two different scientists working independently: the Swedish chemist Carl Scheele and the English clergyman and scientist Joseph Priestley.

⚙ In a 'combustion' reaction, oxygen reacts with another substance (a fuel) to release energy, usually in the form of heat and light.

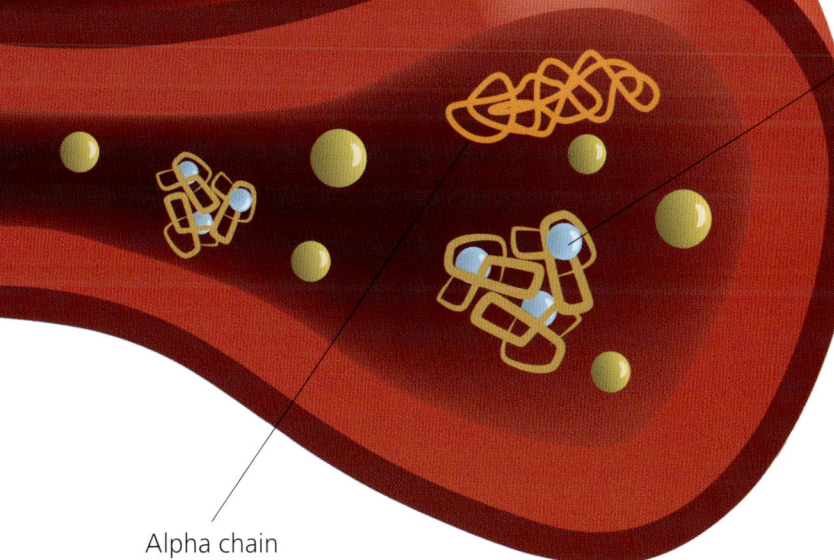

Oxygen

Alpha chain

▶ *Oxygen is needed for combustion to take place.*

Hydrogen

⚙ Hydrogen is the lightest of all gases and elements – a swimming pool full of it would weigh just 1 kg.

⚙ With just one proton and one electron, hydrogen is the first element in the Periodic Table (see page 27).

⚙ Approximately one in every 6,500 hydrogen atoms has a neutron as well as a proton in its nucleus, making it twice as heavy. This atom is called 'deuterium'.

⚙ Some rare hydrogen atoms have two neutrons as well as the proton, making them three times as heavy. These are called 'tritium'.

⚙ The most common substance in the Universe, hydrogen makes up more than 75 per cent of the Universe's mass. It was the first element to form after the Universe began, and billions of years passed before another element formed.

⚙ Most hydrogen on Earth occurs in combination with other elements, such as oxygen in water (H_2O). Pure hydrogen occurs naturally in a few places, such as underground pockets and as tiny traces in the air.

⚙ As one of the most reactive gases, hydrogen is highly flammable.

⚙ Under extreme pressure, hydrogen becomes a metal – the most electrically conductive metal of all.

▲ *The engine beneath the bonnet of this car combines hydrogen in the fuel cell with oxygen – to create a chemical reaction that generates electricity.*

⚙ Most stars contain high levels of hydrogen. Our sun is around 73–75 per cent hydrogen.

⚙ A hydrogen fuel cell creates electrical power from a chemical reaction between hydrogen (the fuel) and oxygen (the oxidant).

⚙ In the future, many cars could be powered by hydrogen fuel cells, which – unlike regular fuels – produce heat and water as by-products, rather than polluting fumes.

⚙ Fuel for hydrogen-powered cars could be made by using solar cells to split water molecules into their component parts (hydrogen and oxygen). Cars powered in this way would be running on a clean mixture of water and sunlight!

◄ *Hydrogen represents about 73–75 per cent of the Sun's mass and up to around 92 per cent of its atoms.*

Nitrogen

⚙ Nitrogen makes up approximately 78 per cent of the air. Like oxygen, it is a colourless, tasteless, odourless gas. Unlike oxygen, nitrogen is inert (unreactive), but it is still vital to organic life.

⚙ Nitrogen becomes liquid at –196°C and freezes at –210°C.

⚙ Liquid nitrogen can be used to freeze substances so quickly that they are practically undamaged by the freezing process.

⚙ Lightning causes reactions between nitrogen and oxygen, resulting in nitrogen oxides (NO_x). NO_x combines with moisture to form many thousands of tonnes of nitric acid per day, which is then washed into soil by rain. This can harm the microorganisms that benefit the soil.

⚙ Compounds of nitrogen are known as nitrates and nitrites. Both are important soil nutrients that help plants to grow healthily.

⚙ During a deep-sea dive, water pressure can cause extra nitrogen to dissolve in the blood. If the diver surfaces too quickly, the nitrogen forms bubbles, causing a dangerous condition known as 'the bends'.

◀ *Nitrogen is a core component of essential biological molecules. Nitrogen-based fertiliser is often added to soil by gardeners and farmers to help improve plant growth.*

Noble gases

⚙ The noble gases are a group of gases that are unreactive. They were given this name because they stay 'nobly' aloof, as if 'uninterested' in creating chemical reactions with other elements.

⚙ Six noble gases occur naturally: helium, neon, argon, krypton, xenon and radon. A seventh, oganesson, was artificially created in 2002.

⚙ All noble gases are unreactive, because their atoms have a full set of electrons in their outer shells. They are tasteless, odourless, colourless and non-flammable.

⚙ Through analysing 'spectral lines' of colour in the Sun's atmosphere, Pierre Janssen and Joseph Lockyer discovered helium in 1868.

⚙ Helium is often used to fill aeronautical balloons and airship bags, because it is much lighter than air but not explosive (like hydrogen).

⚙ Helium is so light that it is able to escape Earth's gravitational pull. When released, helium atoms simply rise through the atmosphere until they escape into the vacuum of space.

⚙ Helium is the second most common element in the Universe, and may make up as much as 24 per cent of the Universe's total mass.

⚙ Neon lights are made by trapping noble gases in a sealed glass tube and then passing an electric current through them to create glowing plasma. Each noble gas creates its own colour, which is enhanced by fluorescent coatings on the glass.

▶ *These glowing, illuminated signs are made from sealed glass tubes filled with noble gases.*

Carbon

⚙ Carbon is the fourth most abundant element in the Universe after hydrogen, helium and oxygen. Most of it was originally built inside stars.

⚙ Carbon atoms have space for four electrons in their outer shells, which gives carbon the ability to form many millions of different compounds.

⚙ Pure carbon occurs in five major allotropes (forms). These are: diamond, graphite, amorphous carbon, fullerenes and carbon nanotubes.

⚙ Diamond, graphite and amorphous carbon form naturally, while fullerenes and carbon nanotubes are usually created artificially.

⚙ Carbon has the highest melting point of all elements. The melting point of diamond is around 3,550°C, but carbon usually 'sublimes' (goes straight from solid to gas), at around 3,630°C.

⚙ Graphite is the black carbon used in pencils. Its atoms are arranged in sheets that slide over each other, so it is quite soft.

⚙ Carbon nanotubes are tubes of carbon atoms measuring a few nanometres across (a nanometre is a billionth of a metre). They are 20 times as strong as steel, and can bend and conduct electricity around 1,000 times better than copper.

▶ *Natural diamond is one of the world's hardest substances, forged by pressure deep down in the Earth billions of years ago.*

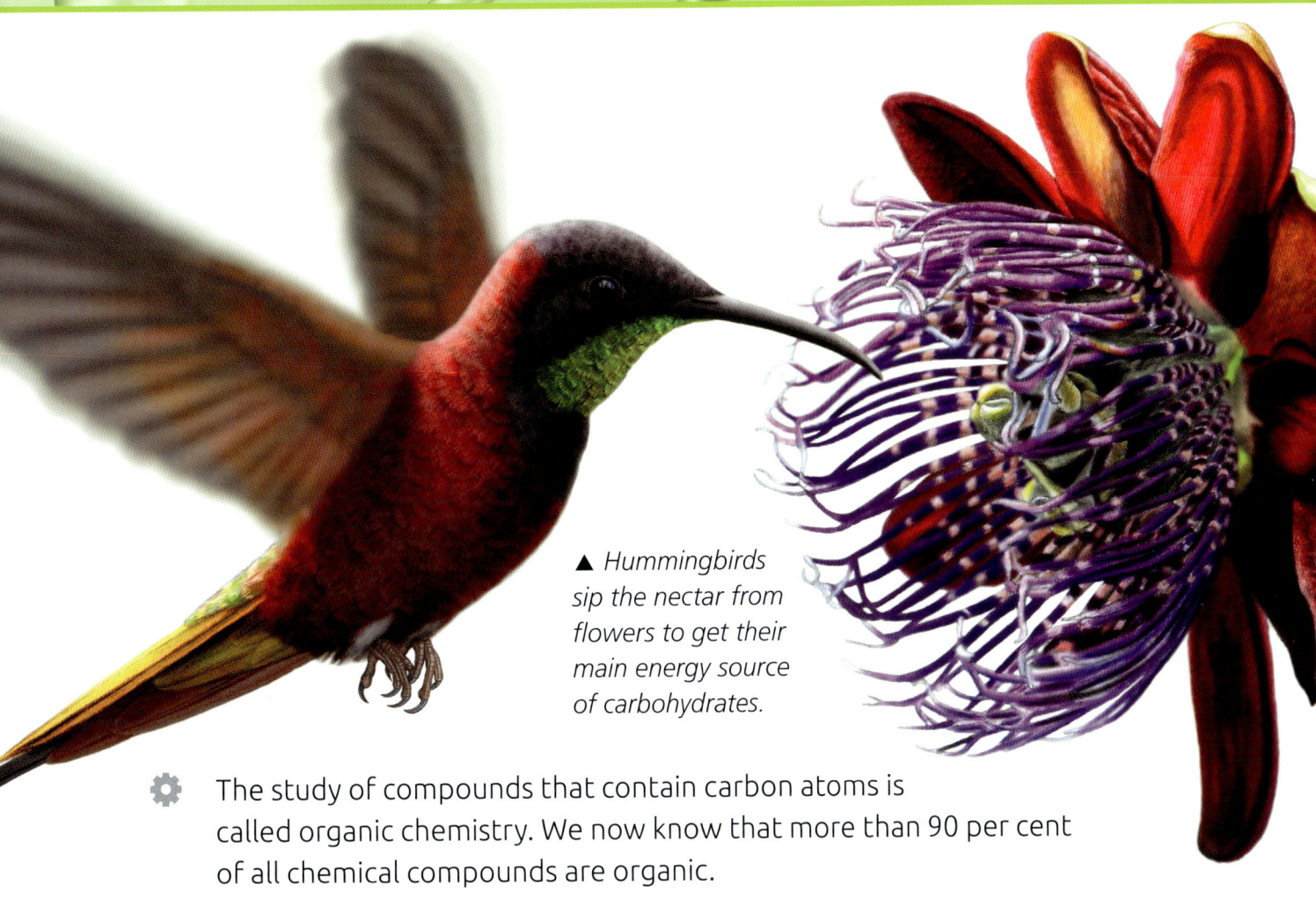

▲ *Hummingbirds sip the nectar from flowers to get their main energy source of carbohydrates.*

⚙ The study of compounds that contain carbon atoms is called organic chemistry. We now know that more than 90 per cent of all chemical compounds are organic.

⚙ Most organic compounds consist of carbon and hydrogen, often combined with other elements such as nitrogen, oxygen, phosphorus and silicon. Compounds that consist of hydrogen and carbon are called 'hydrocarbons'. These are the largest groups of carbon compounds.

⚙ There are many natural hydrocarbons in the human body, including steroid hormones such as testosterone and cholesterol, which helps in the construction of blood vessel walls.

⚙ Hydrocarbons and carbohydrates are not the same. Hydrocarbons are made from carbon and hydrogen atoms, while carbohydrates contain oxygen atoms as well. This enables carbohydrates to take a huge variety of forms – all essential for life.

⚙ Carbohydrates such as starches and sugars are the basic energy foods of plants and animals.

43

Oil

⚙ Oils are liquids that burn easily and do not dissolve in water. They are usually made from groups of carbon and hydrogen atoms. There are three main types of oil: essential oils, fixed oils and mineral oils.

⚙ Essential oils are thin, highly perfumed oils derived (taken) from plants. They are used in food flavouring and aromatherapy.

⚙ Fixed oils, such as fish or nut oils, are derived from plants and animals.

⚙ Mineral oils are derived from petroleum, which is formed underground over millions of years from the remains of tiny marine organisms such as plankton.

⚙ Petroleum is a mixture of organic compounds, most of which are hydrocarbons, combined with small amounts of other elements, including oxygen, sulphur and nitrogen.

⚙ Petroleum is separated into different substances – such as aviation fuel, petrol and paraffin – through distillation (see page 17).

⚙ There are different forms of petroleum, such as crude oil and natural gas. Crude oil is usually thick and sticky, but it can vary in its composition and colour, from jet-black Sudan oil to straw-coloured Texas oil.

▶ *Oil forms in the ground over millions of years from the remains of microscopic sea creatures.*

⚙ The simplest hydrocarbon is methane (CH_4), the main gas in natural gas. As its chemical formula shows, methane molecules are composed of one carbon atom and four hydrogen atoms.

⚙ There are three main types of hydrocarbon in oil – alkanes, aromatics and naphthenes. The proportion of each varies from oil to oil.

⚙ Lighter alkanes are gases such as methane, propane and butane (used in camping stoves). Candles contain a mixture of alkanes. Alkanes generally make good fuels, as they give off lots of light and heat energy when they combust.

⚙ Alkenes are also hydrocarbons. The simplest alkene is ethene, also known as ethylene (C_2H_4), which is used to make plastics. It is the basis of many paint strippers and can be used to make ethanol – the alcohol in drinks such as wine.

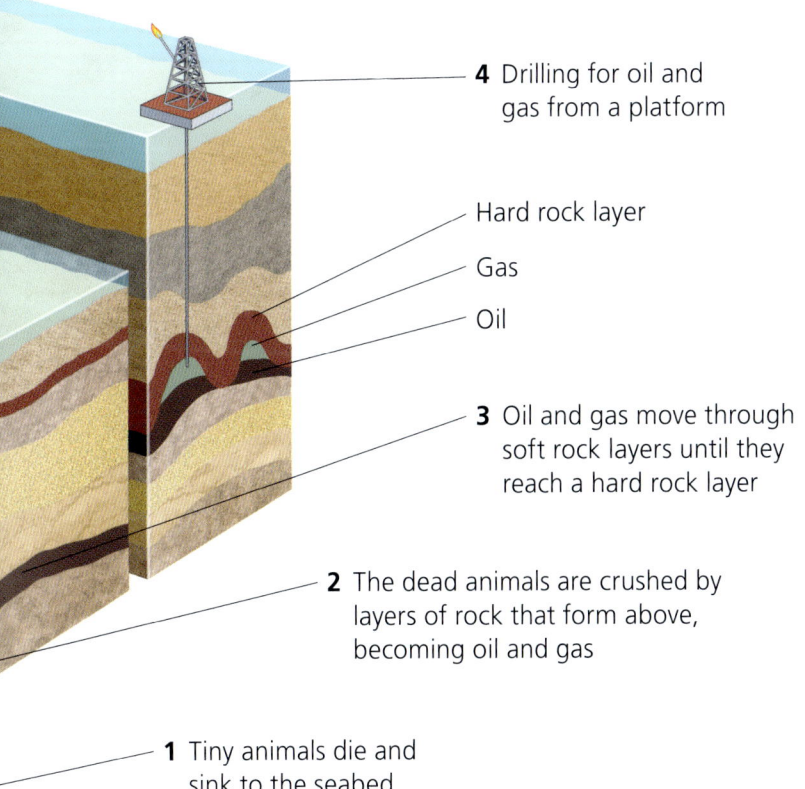

4 Drilling for oil and gas from a platform

Hard rock layer

Gas

Oil

3 Oil and gas move through soft rock layers until they reach a hard rock layer

2 The dead animals are crushed by layers of rock that form above, becoming oil and gas

1 Tiny animals die and sink to the seabed

DID YOU KNOW?
Petroleum is used to make a huge range of products, from aspirin and toothpaste to cosmetics (make-up).

◀ *Crude oil is found in pressurised pockets deep beneath the Earth's surface. When one of these is breached by drilling, the oil can shoot out – dozens of metres into the sky.*

Synthetic materials

⚙ Materials that are human-made, rather than occurring naturally, are known as 'synthetic'.

⚙ Many synthetic materials, such as plastics, are polymers – substances with long chains of organic molecules that are made up from lots of identical, smaller molecules called monomers.

⚙ The first synthetic polymer was Parkesine. It was invented by Alexander Parkes in 1862.

⚙ The polymer nylon was the first completely synthetic fibre. It was created by Wallace Carothers of DuPont (an American chemical company) in the 1930s, and was used to make everything from stockings to toothbrushes.

⚙ Kevlar is a fibre, developed by Stephanie Kwolek of DuPont in the 1960s, based on aromatic polymers. Kevlar is so light and tough it can be specially woven to help make bullet-proof vests.

⚙ Composites are new, strong, lightweight materials, created by combining a polymer with another 'strengthening' material (such as carbon fibres).

⚙ Plastics are synthetic materials that can be easily shaped and moulded. Most plastics are polymers. A plastic gets its properties from the way its polymer molecules are arranged.

⚙ Long chains of molecules that slide over each other easily make flexible plastics, whereas angled chains create rigid plastics.

◀ *This competitive sprinter is able to run with the use of two carbon-fibre 'running-specific prostheses' (or RSPs).*

⚙ Many plastics are made out of compounds extracted from crude oil.

⚙ Thermoplastics are soft and mouldable when warm, but set solid when cool. They are used to make products such as bottles and drainpipes. Thermoset plastics, which cannot be remelted once set, are used to make products such as telephones and pan handles.

⚙ Polyvinyl chloride (PVC) is a hard plastic, so it is used to make window frames. It can also be softened with 'plasticizers' to make anything from shoes to shampoo bottles.

⚙ Polycarbonate is resistant to chemicals, so it is used to make containers for medicines and industrial chemicals.

⚙ Plastics do not decompose in the same way that organic matter does. It can take hundreds of years for plastics to break down into smaller particles of plastic. These tiny particles are called microplastics.

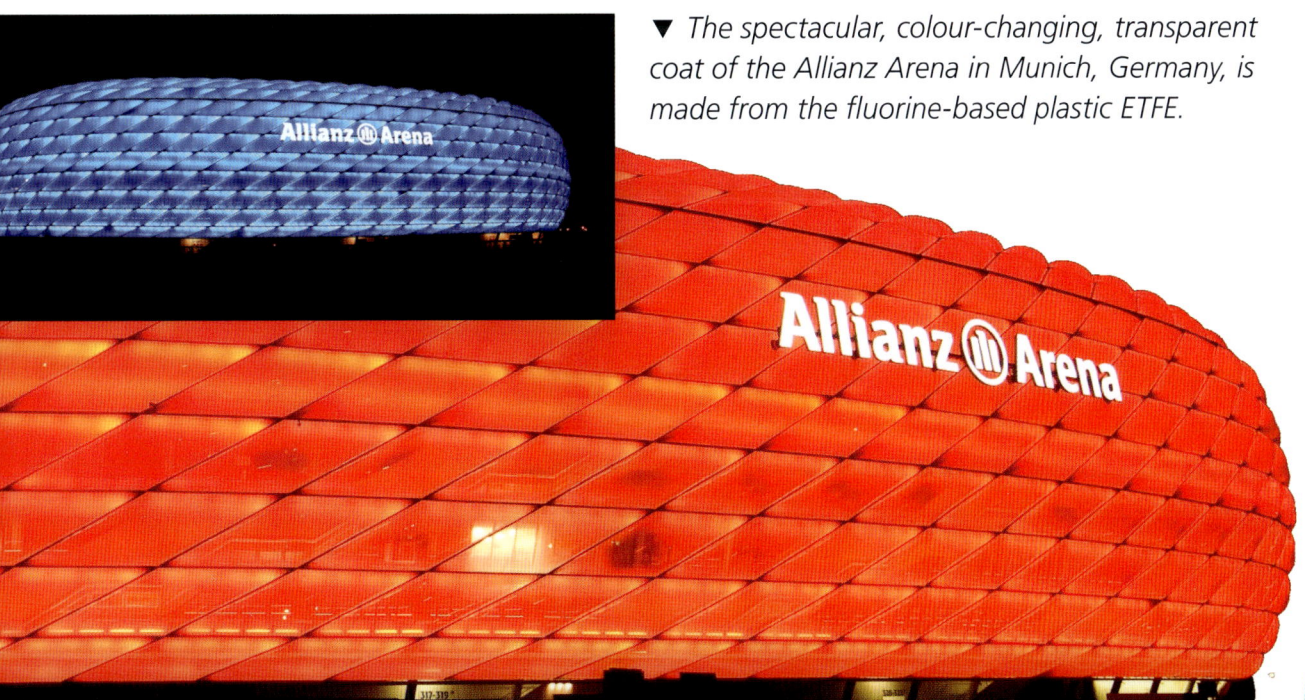

▼ *The spectacular, colour-changing, transparent coat of the Allianz Arena in Munich, Germany, is made from the fluorine-based plastic ETFE.*

Glass

⚙ Most human-made glass is created by heating together sand, soda ash (sodium carbonate) and limestone (calcium carbonate).

⚙ Silica is a hard, glassy solid found in sand. Glass can be made from silica alone, but it has a very high melting point (of around 1,700°C), so soda ash is added to lower its melting point. Adding a lot of soda ash makes glass too soluble in water, so limestone is added to reduce its solubility.

⚙ To make sheets of glass, 6 per cent lime and 4 per cent magnesia (or magnesium oxide) are added to the mix.

⚙ To make glass for bottles, 2 per cent alumina (or aluminium oxide) is added to the basic mix.

⚙ The cheapest glass is green because it contains iron impurities. Metallic oxides are added to the mix to make different colours.

⚙ Unlike most solids, glass is amorphous (not made of crystals) so it does not have the same rigid structure as other solids.

◄ *When glass is extremely hot, it flows slowly, like a thick liquid. Molten (liquid) glass is shaped by 'glass-blowing', the process of adding air into it through a tube.*

DID YOU KNOW?
The unusual molecular structure of glass means that it is considered neither a true solid nor a liquid, but an 'amorphous solid'.

✿ While most glass that we are familar with is made in a glassworks, it can also form naturally.

✿ Obsidian is also known as 'volcanic' glass. It is formed by the rapid cooling of silica-rich lava. Obsidian is usually jet black in colour, and has been used historically for making weapons and tools.

✿ Fulgurites, also known as fossilised lightning, are a type of glass formed when lightning strikes silca-rich sand. Water trapped between the grains conducts the electricity, which superheats the sand, causing it to fuse together into tube-like structures.

✿ Rock fulgurites form as 'veins' of glass in rock, where it has been struck by lightning. Mountain peaks often act as lightning rods, which is why rock fulgurites can be found in most mountain ranges.

✿ Some ocean creatures, such as sea sponges, are made of glass. They use materials such as silica to form the needlelike structures (known as spicules) that make up their skeletons.

✿ NASA has found evidence that it may rain molten glass on an exoplanet known as HD 189733b. The whole planet shows up as a bright blue colour, due to starlight reflecting off of its silica-rich clouds.

◄ *HD 189733b is a huge gas giant with scorching atmospheric temperatures of over 1,000°C, where it rains molten glass, sideways, in howling 7,000-kilometre-per-hour winds.*

49

Air

⚙ Air is a mixture of gases, dust and moisture.

⚙ The gas nitrogen makes up around 78 per cent of the air on earth. Nitrogen is usually unreactive, but sometimes reacts with oxygen to form nitrogen oxides.

⚙ Oxygen makes up about 21 per cent of the air. Animals breathe in oxygen, while plants give it out as they take their energy from sunlight in photosynthesis.

⚙ Earth's atmosphere began to gain oxygen from the billions of plantlike microorganisms that floated in the oceans over two billion years ago.

⚙ The air contains very small quantities of the inert gases argon, neon, helium, krypton and xenon.

⚙ It also contains a number of more reactive gases, including carbon dioxide, water vapour, ozone, sulphur dioxide and nitrogen dioxide.

▼ *Earth's atmosphere has a series of different layers. As you move from the troposphere outwards, to the exosphere, the air gets thinner and Earth's gravity is more weakly felt.*

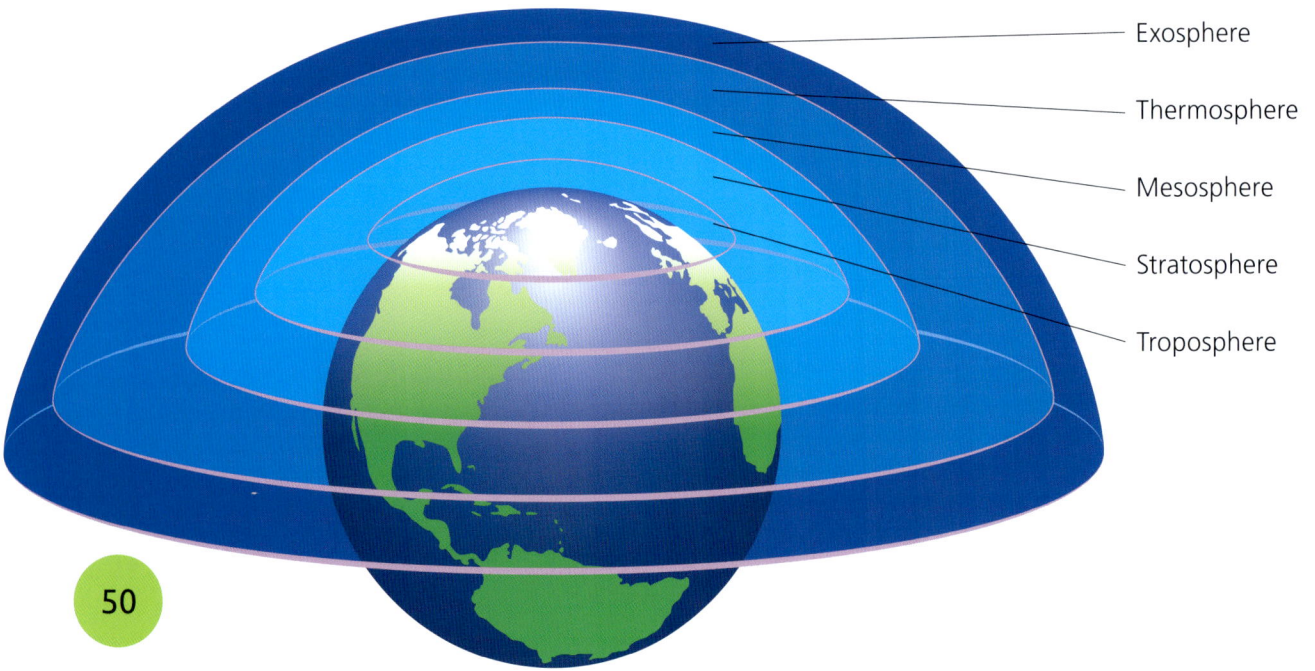

Exosphere

Thermosphere

Mesosphere

Stratosphere

Troposphere

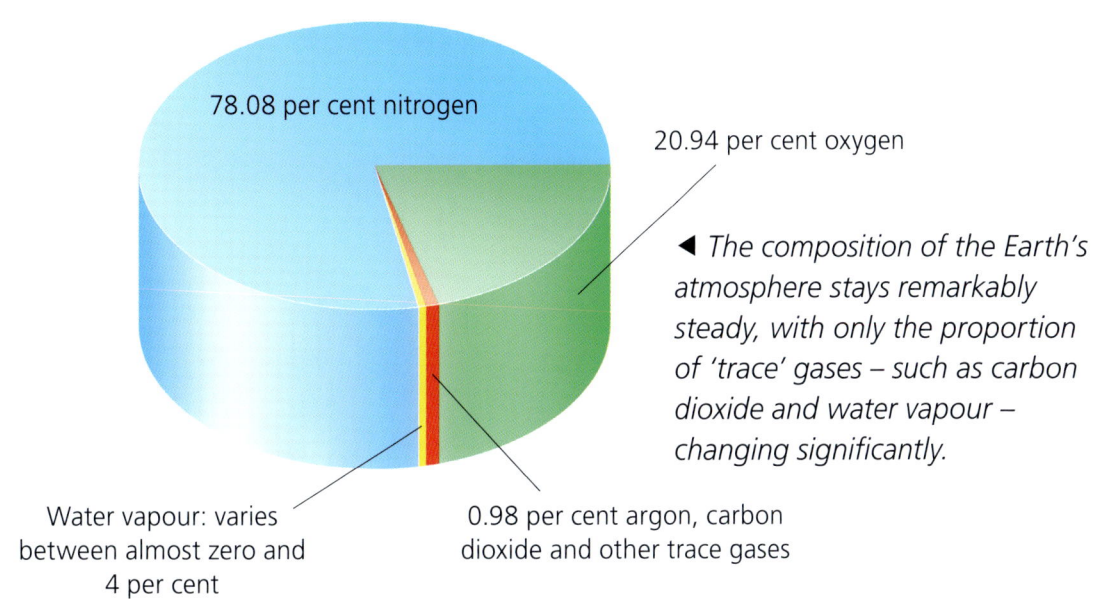

78.08 per cent nitrogen

20.94 per cent oxygen

◀ *The composition of the Earth's atmosphere stays remarkably steady, with only the proportion of 'trace' gases – such as carbon dioxide and water vapour – changing significantly.*

Water vapour: varies between almost zero and 4 per cent

0.98 per cent argon, carbon dioxide and other trace gases

⚙ Carbon dioxide (CO_2) makes up approximately 0.04 per cent of the air. This gas is being continually recycled as it is breathed out by animals and taken in by plants through the process of photosynthesis.

⚙ Ozone makes up around 0.00006 per cent of the air. It is created when sunlight breaks up oxygen. Hydrogen makes up 0.00005 per cent of the air, and some of it very slowly drifts off into space.

⚙ Air is typically polluted with gases, tiny solid particles (such as soot or microplastics) and aerosols (tiny droplets suspended in a gas).

⚙ Some pollution is natural, such as dust from storms, soot and smoke from forest fires and ash from volcanic eruptions. However, a lot of pollution is created by human activities, including exhaust fumes from vehicles and emissions from factories and power stations.

⚙ Methane belched out by cows and the CO_2 created by burning oil and coal are known as 'greenhouse gases'. The emissions of greenhouse gases are one of the driving forces contributing to climate change.

⚙ Air is 'thinner' at high altitudes, meaning there is less oxygen and less air pressure. This is because, as you get further away from the centre of the planet, the pull of its gravity on gas molecules is weaker. This makes the atmosphere less dense.

Water

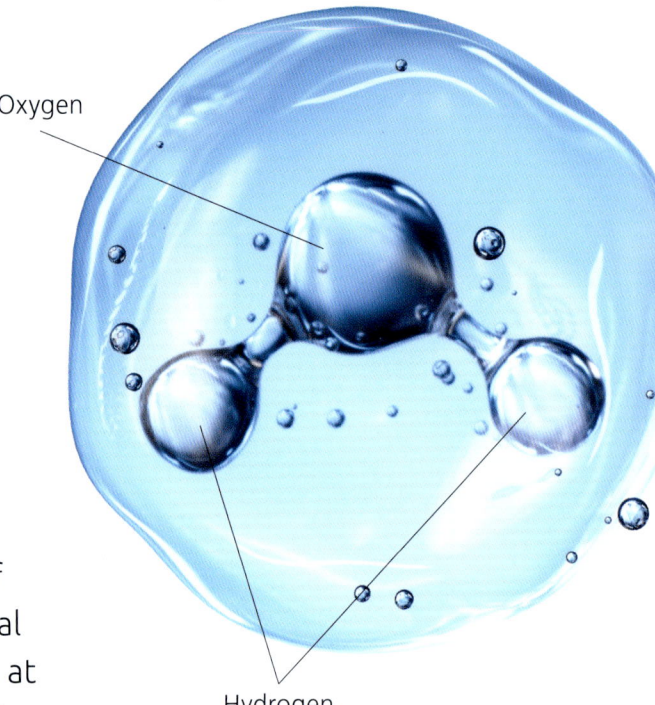

Oxygen

Hydrogen

▲ *Water's V-shaped molecule has an oxygen atom (top) at its base and a hydrogen atom (bottom) at each tip.*

- Water is a compound made of two hydrogen atoms and one oxygen atom. It has the chemical formula H_2O. A water molecule is shaped like a flattened letter 'V', with the two hydrogen atoms at each tip.

- Water is the only substance that commonly exists in all three states of matter (solid, liquid and gas) at normal temperatures and pressures. It melts at around 0°C and boils at around 100°C.

- The boiling point of water varies according to atmospheric pressure. It is 100°C at sea level, but just 68°C at the top of Mount Everest (Earth's highest point above sea level), where air pressure is much lower.

- Ice is much less dense than water, which is why ice floats.

- Water is one of the few substances that expands as it freezes, which is why pipes burst during cold weather.

- Water stays in a liquid form until 100°C, because pairs of its 'polar' molecules make strong bonds, as the positively charged end of one molecule is drawn to the negatively charged end of another.

- The way in which water molecules are drawn together creates a lot of surface tension. This is what pulls water drops into globules.

- Water covers approximately 71 per cent of the Earth's surface. Most of this is in the oceans and rivers, while around 1.6 per cent of all water is in the ground and approximately 0.001 per cent of it is in the air as vapour, clouds and rain.

⚙ Some of the world's water (just over 2 per cent of it) is frozen as glaciers and ice caps, but global warming may reduce this proportion.

⚙ Liquid water may occur elsewhere in space – in small amounts on the Moon; under the surface of Enceladus, one of Saturn's moons; and on Europa, one of Jupiter's moons. Water ice is known to be present on Mars, as well as on Titan, Saturn's largest moon.

▲ *NASA's Curiosity rover captured images of Marker Band Valley on Mars in 2022. The rippled rock textures found in this area provide clear evidence that liquid water moved across the Martian surface – in an ancient, shallow lake – around 3.7 billion years ago.*

Weight and mass

⚙ Mass is the amount of matter, or 'stuff', in an object. Mass is not the same as weight. In physics, 'weight' refers to the force of gravity acting on an object. An object's weight varies according to its mass and the strength of the gravitational field it happens to be in.

⚙ Objects weigh more at sea level, which is nearer the centre of the Earth, than they do when at high altitude – such as at the top of a mountain.

⚙ If you were standing on the Moon, you would weigh only one-sixth of your weight on Earth, because the Moon's gravity is one-sixth of the Earth's gravity.

⚙ The weight of an object can vary, but its mass is always the same, so scientists use units of mass (such as kilograms, or kg) to measure the amount of matter (or 'stuff') a substance contains.

◄ *Here, American astronaut Drew Feustel is on a spacewalk, tethered to the International Space Station. Both are in a state of continuous 'free fall' as they move in orbit, at high speed, around the Earth. This creates a state of 'microgravity', in which objects and astronauts float around as if they have very little weight.*

⚙ The mass of the Earth is 6 x 10^{24} (six trillion trillion) kg.

⚙ Density is the measure of how much matter is packed into a certain space (volume), or how tightly the particles in a substance are packed together. It is measured in units such as grams per cubic centimetre (g/cm^3).

DID YOU KNOW?
The largest stars in the galaxy have a mass 150 times bigger than the Sun – that's 3 x 10^{32} kg.

▼ *Experimental aircraft are used to train astronauts, enabling them to experience the effects of microgravity before spending time in Earth's orbit.*

⚙ The lightest known, lowest-density solids are silica aerogels, made for space science, which have a density of approximately 0.005 g/cm^3.

⚙ The lightest known element is hydrogen. As a gas, it has a density of around 0.00008989 g/cm^3. The density of air is 0.00128 g/cm^3.

⚙ The densest solid is osmium, at 22.59 g/cm^3. Lead is 11.37 g/cm^3. A neutron star has a density of about one billion trillion g/cm^3.

Inertia and momentum

⚙ Inertia is the property that causes a body to resist any change in speed caused by a force. For example, a ball on a level surface doesn't move because inertia keeps it where it is. A push or kick provides the force to make it move.

⚙ Momentum is an object's mass multiplied by its velocity (the rate at which it moves in a particular direction).

⚙ Inertia and momentum depend on mass. A large force is needed to slow down or speed up an object that has lots of mass.

⚙ When a moving object strikes another object (when you kick a ball, for example), the momentum of the moving object (your foot) is transferred to the object it strikes (the ball), making it move. This is known as the 'law of conservation of momentum'.

▼ *Baseball players twist their bodies when preparing to hit a ball. This allows them to generate a greater velocity, so that they can hit the ball with more momentum.*

▲ *This crushed car shows the damage that can be caused by the force of momentum when objects collide. Car manufacturers routinely test how their cars perform during a crash, so that they can maximise the safety of the passengers.*

⚙ The momentum of a spinning object is called angular momentum. When a spinning skater draws their arms close in to their body, their spin diameter (the circle they are making) is smaller than it would be if their arms were outstretched. To conserve the angular momentum (keep it going), the skater's body automatically spins faster.

⚙ For the same reason, a satellite orbiting closer to the Earth travels faster than one orbiting farther out.

⚙ Newton's Cradle is a small device composed of multiple metal balls on individual strings, suspended in a line. When one ball is swung against the others, conservation of momentum results in the ball at the other end of the sequence swinging outwards in response.

DID YOU KNOW?
The word 'inertia' comes from the Latin word 'iners', which means 'inactive' or 'sluggish'.

Motion

⚙ Every movement in the Universe is governed by laws. The three most important laws were described by English scientist Isaac Newton.

⚙ Newton's first law of motion states that an object accelerates, slows down or changes direction only when a force is acting on it.

⚙ Newton's second law of motion states that the acceleration of an object depends on how massive the object is, and on the size of the force that is acting on it.

⚙ Newton's third law of motion states that, when a force acts in one way, an equal force acts in the opposite way. 'To every action, there is an equal and opposite reaction'.

⚙ Rocket engines depend on Newton's law. As the hot gases shoot out of the rocket motors (the action), the rocket reacts against them and is propelled forwards (the reaction).

⚙ Reactions are not always visible. When you bounce a ball on the ground, only the ball appears to move, but the ground recoils as well. It is virtually impossible for our eyes to detect the Earth's recoil, however, because its mass is huge compared to that of the ball.

⚙ When an object is moving in one direction at a constant speed, it is described as having 'uniform velocity'.

⚙ The speed of the travelling object can be worked out using the following formula:

$$\frac{\text{distance travelled (d)}}{\text{time (t)}} = \text{velocity (v)}$$

▲ *Electric motors accelerate this Japanese*
'bullet train' to speeds of more than 300 km/h.

⚙ Acceleration is the rate of change of velocity. When something speeds
up (accelerates), it has positive acceleration. When something slows
down (decelerates), it has negative acceleration.

⚙ Acceleration can be measured in metres per second squared (m/sec^2).
This means that, in each passing second, speed increases or decreases
by so many metres per second. A rifle bullet accelerates down its barrel
at approximately 3,000 m/sec^2. A fast car accelerates at 6 m/sec^2.

⚙ Earth's gravitational pull causes freely falling objects to accelerate.
The rate at which this happens is known as 'g' (standard acceleration
due to gravity). Near to the Earth's surface, this rate is 9.8 m/sec^2.

⚙ A plane takes off at around 0.5 g, while a car brakes at up to 0.7 g.
In a car crash, humans may survive a deceleration of up to 100 g.

Forces

⚙ A force is a push or a pull. It can make something start to move, slow down, speed up, change direction or change its shape or size. The greater the force, the more effect it has.

⚙ Force is measured in newtons (N). One newton is the force needed to speed up a mass of one kilogram by 1 m/sec^2 (or by one metre per second, every second).

⚙ When an object moves, there are usually several forces involved. For example, when you throw a ball, the force of your throw hurls it forwards, the force of gravity pulls it down – and the force of air resistance slows it down.

⚙ The direction and speed of any movement depends on the combined effect of all the forces involved, which is known as the 'resultant' force (or net force).

◀ *A roller coaster gets its speed from gravity. As the gravitational pull takes it downhill, the stored gravitational 'potential energy' is transformed into 'kinetic' (movement) energy as the cars accelerate.*

⚙ A force has magnitude (size) and works in a particular direction.

⚙ A force can be drawn on a diagram as an arrow, known as a vector. The arrow's direction shows the force's direction and its length indicates the force's strength.

⚙ Four fundamental forces operate throughout the Universe. These are: gravity, the electromagnetic force, the strong nuclear force and the weak nuclear force.

⚙ A force field is the area affected by a force. The field is strongest in the region closest to the source of the force.

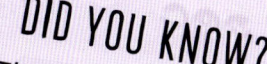

DID YOU KNOW?
The thrust of NASA's Saturn V rocket engines, used for the Apollo Moon missions, was equal to 33 million newtons.

▼ *When this boxer hits a punchball, the ball is moved by the force of his punch.*

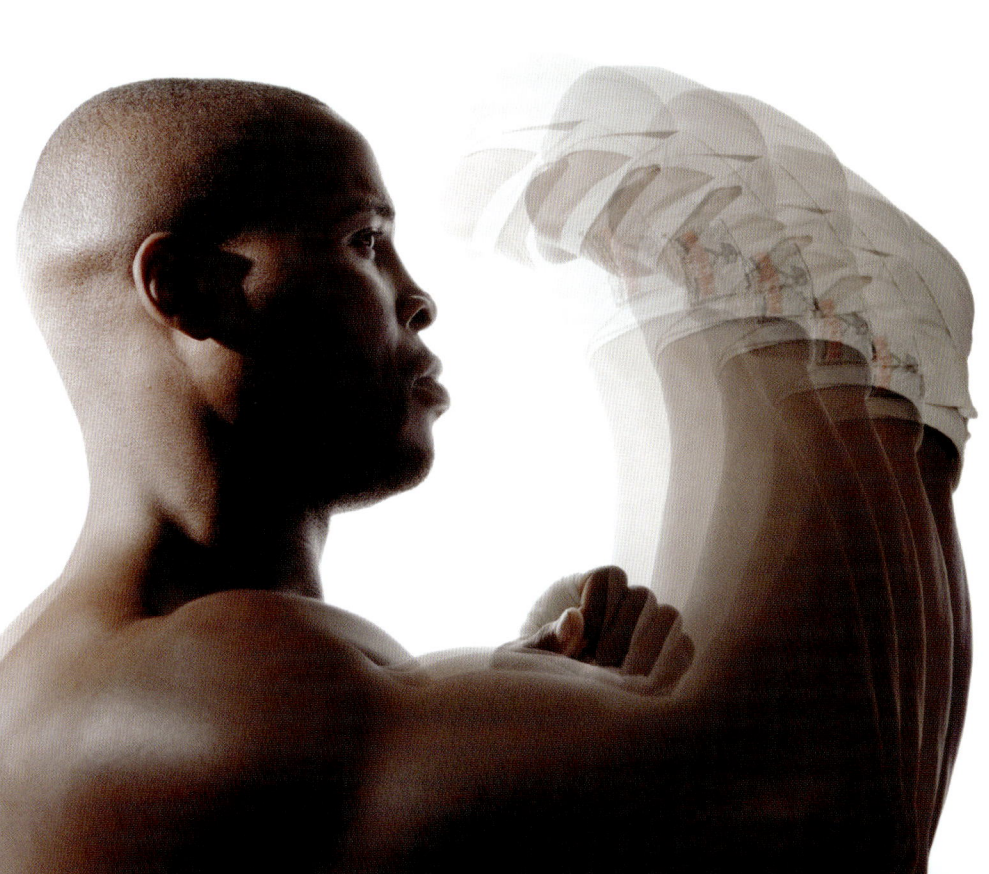

61

Machines

⚙ In science, a machine is a device that reduces the effort needed to move a load by modifying the force applied or changing its direction.

⚙ Forces always act in straight lines, but when a force acts on an object that pivots around a fixed point (a fulcrum), it creates a turning effect.

⚙ The size of the turning effect is called the 'moment' by physicists and 'torque' by engineers. The further from the fulcrum the force is applied, the greater the moment.

⚙ Simple machines often use turning effects to improve their power. Levers, gears and pulleys are simple machines that can be combined to make complex machines, such as cars.

⚙ A lever is a simple machine consisting of a rigid bar that pivots about a fulcrum somewhere along its length.

⚙ A gear is a simple machine that transmits (passes on) motion through multiple rotating, toothed wheels.

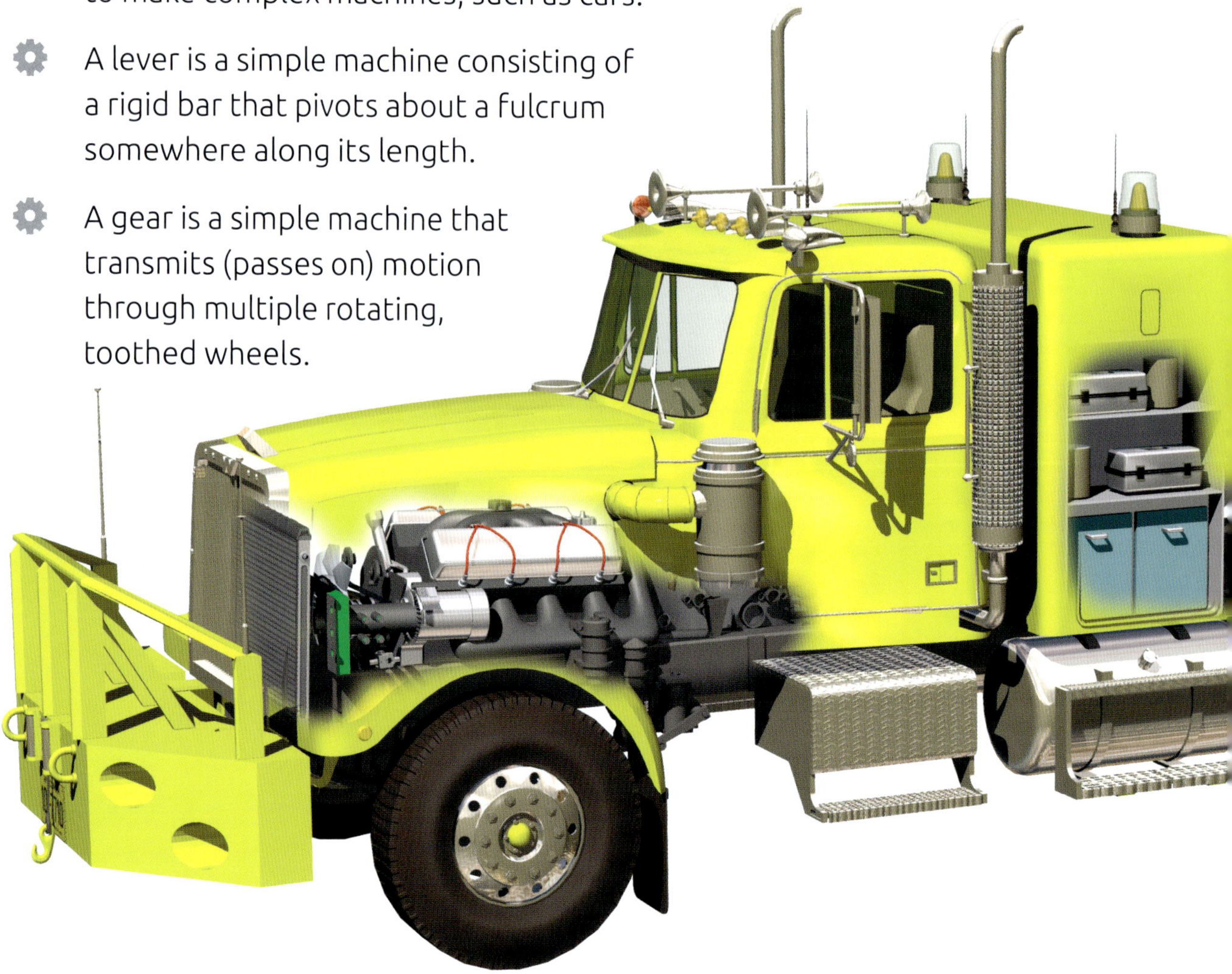

⚙ The mechanical advantage (MA) is a measure of how effective a machine is in terms of 'amplifying' a force. It indicates the relationship between a load and the effort required to move it (using the machine).

⚙ The velocity ratio (VR) is the distance moved by the effort, divided by the distance moved by the load.

⚙ In a perfect machine, the VR would match the MA, but most machines are inefficient, with losses occurring between the effort and the load due to forces such as friction.

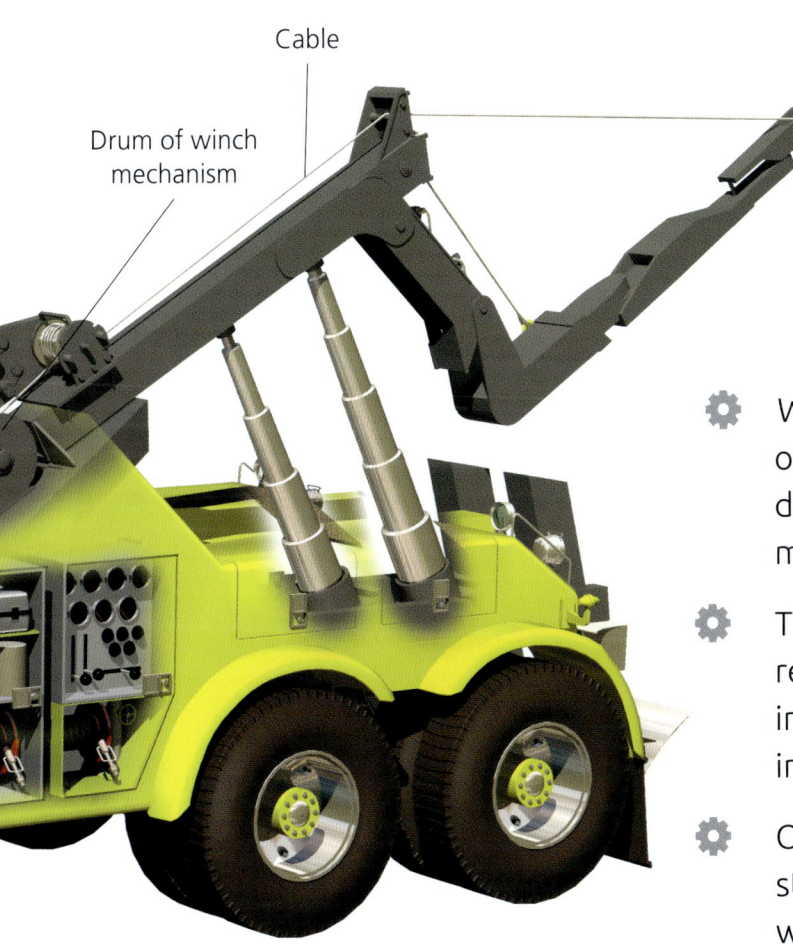

Cable

Drum of winch mechanism

◄ *Breakdown trucks have a strong cable attached to a winch, which is a giant pulley. The operator can attach the large hook at the end of the cable to a broken-down car, and slowly wind the cable into the spool or drum.*

⚙ Whenever a force moves an object, scientists say 'work' is done. Work is the force applied multiplied by the distance moved.

⚙ The efficiency of a machine is the relationship between 'work done in moving the load' and 'work involved in applying the effort'.

⚙ One of the earliest machines still in use today is a screwlike, water-lifting device called a dalu, first used in Sumeria around 5,500 years ago.

Stretching and pulling

⚙ Elasticity is the degree to which a solid can return to its original size and shape after being stretched, squeezed or deformed (misshapen).

⚙ A force that misshapes a material is called a stress. The amount that a solid is stretched or squeezed when under stress is known as 'strain'.

⚙ All solids have some elasticity, but some – such as rubber, nylon and coiled springs – are very elastic. A solid will return to its original shape when the stress stops, as long as the stress does not exceed its elastic limit – the point at which a material loses elasticity (and cannot return to its original form).

⚙ The amount by which a solid stretches under a particular force – the ratio of stress to strain – is known as its 'elastic modulus'.

⚙ Solids with a low elastic modulus, such as rubber, are more flexible and stretch easily. Solids with a high elastic modulus, such as steel, are more rigid and resist stretching.

DID YOU KNOW?
Some types of rubber can be stretched 1,000 times beyond their original length before reaching their elastic limit.

◄ *The leverage of the bow string helps an archer to bend the elastic material of the bow – so that it can transfer tremendous power to the arrow as it snaps back into shape.*

Pressure

⚙ Pressure is force applied to a surface. It is measured as the force acting 'per unit area' of a surface. The standard unit of pressure is the pascal (Pa) or 1 newton per square metre (N/m^2).

⚙ The pressure at the centre of the Earth may be 400 billion Pa. Steel can withstand 40 million Pa, while a shark bite may reach 30 million Pa.

⚙ Pressure from a gas or liquid is actually the assault of fast-moving molecules on surfaces around or within it.

⚙ An inflated bicycle tyre feels firm because of the constant battering of air molecules against the inside of the tyre. Pumping pushes more air molecules into the available space, and so increases the pressure.

⚙ Pressures are greater in liquids than in gases because liquids are more dense.

⚙ The deeper you go into the ocean, the greater are the weight and pressure of the water above you: 10,000 m below the surface is equivalent to seven elephants standing on a plate.

⚙ Air pressure outside your body is balanced by the pressure of fluids and tissues inside your body. Without this internal pressure, air pressure would crush your body instantly.

▶ *Balloons remain inflated because the pressure of the gas inside them is greater than the pressure of the surrounding air.*

65

Floating and sinking

⚙ When an object is placed in liquid, its weight displaces (pushes away) a volume of the liquid. The displaced liquid pushes back on the solid with a force called 'upthrust'.

⚙ If the upthrust is equal to or greater than the object's weight, the object will float. This is known as Archimedes' principle.

⚙ So, an object is technically 'sinking' until its weight is equal to the upthrust of the water, at which point it floats. The ability of an object to float is called 'buoyancy'.

⚙ An object will only float if its average density (see page 55) is the same or less than the liquid surrounding it.

⚙ A steel ship can float, even though steel is denser than water, because its hull is full of air. The massive ship will sink to a point where enough water is displaced to match the combined weight of the steel and the air inside the hull – and then it will float.

⚙ Ships float at different heights according to how heavily they are laden and how dense the surrounding water is. They tend to float higher in seawater than in fresh water, because the salts dissolved into seawater make it more dense.

▼ *Submarines can control their buoyancy using ballast tanks:* **1** *When they need to dive, submariners open the ballast tanks and allow them to fill with water.* **2** *This increases the submarine's density, allowing it to sink.* **3** *Releasing compressed air into the ballast tanks forces the water out again, enabling the vessel to rise or surface.*

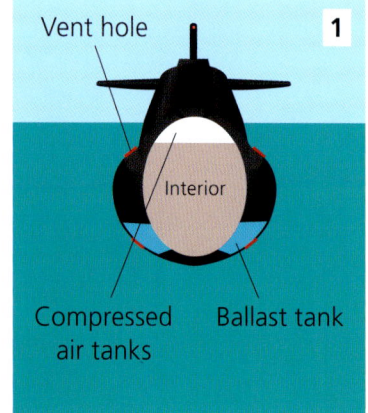
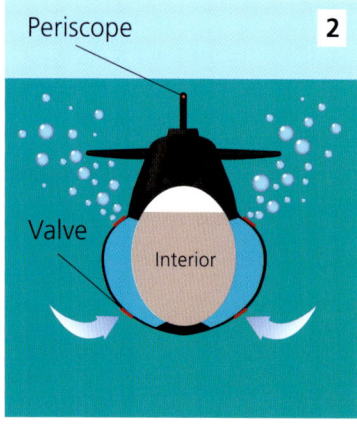

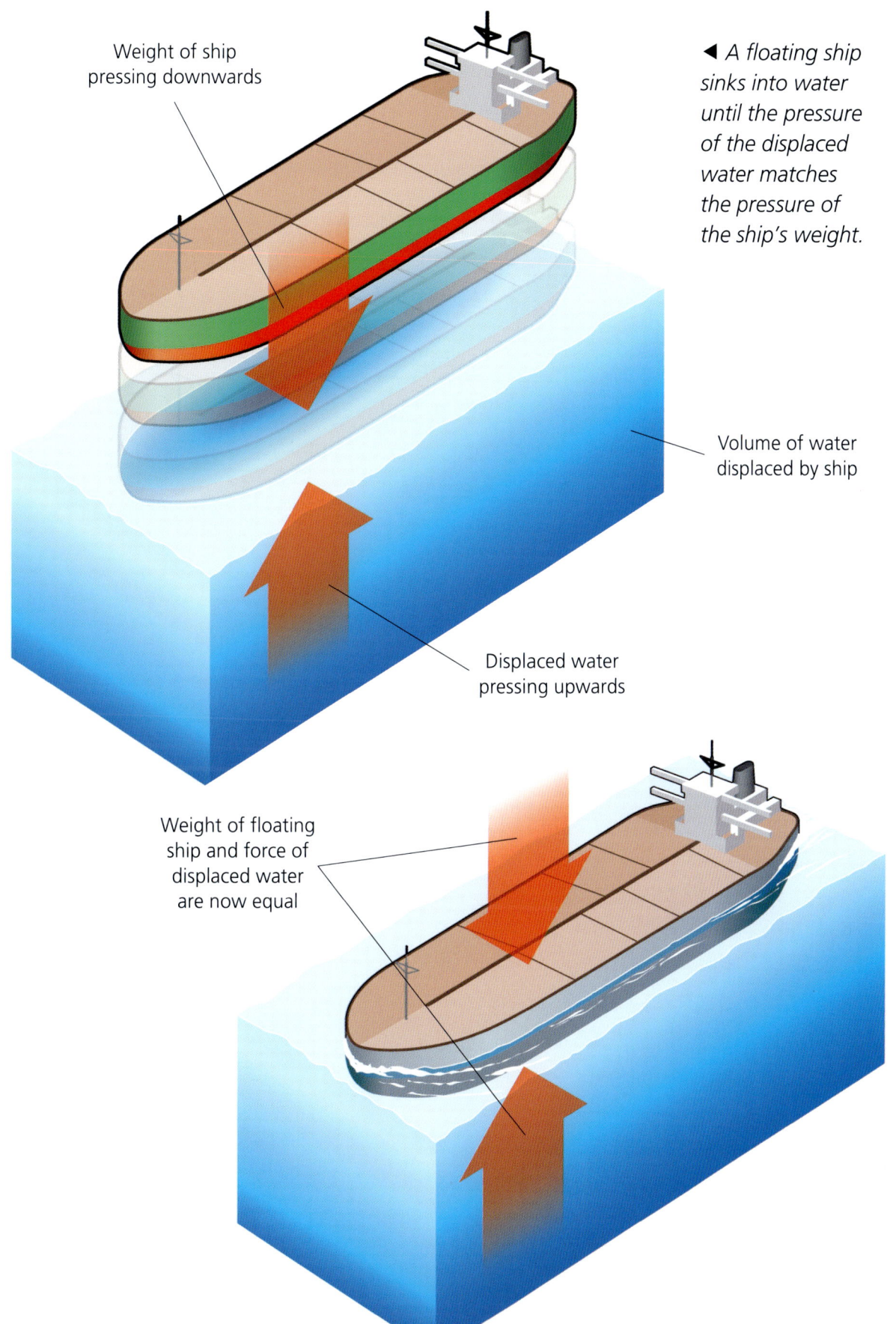

Weight of ship pressing downwards

◀ *A floating ship sinks into water until the pressure of the displaced water matches the pressure of the ship's weight.*

Volume of water displaced by ship

Displaced water pressing upwards

Weight of floating ship and force of displaced water are now equal

67

Energy

⚙ Energy is the capacity of a system to do work. It has many forms, known as energy stores, ranging from the chemical energy locked in sugar to the mechanical energy in a speeding train.

⚙ Energy conversion occurs when energy changes from one store to another. When energy moves from one place to another it is known as energy transfer.

⚙ Energy is never lost or gained, it simply changes or moves. The total amount of energy in the Universe has always been the same. Using energy usually means converting it from one store to another.

⚙ Potential energy is energy that is stored up within a body or system, ready for action. The energy stored in a coiled spring is an example of potential energy.

⚙ Kinetic energy is energy that is possessed by an object because it is moving. A rolling ball has kinetic energy.

⚙ The greater an object's mass or velocity, the greater its kinetic energy. A car has four times more kinetic energy at 40 km/h than at 20 km/h.

◄ *Inside the Sun, nuclear energy stored in atoms is converted into heat energy, making the surface ferociously hot.*

Converting energy

⚙ Energy is measured in joules (J). One J is equal to the amount of energy involved in moving a force of 1 newton (N) over a distance of 1 m. A kilojoule (kJ) equals 1,000 J.

⚙ Energy used to be measured in calories, but these are now used only when referring to the energy content of food. One calorie is approximately 4.2 J. One kilocalorie (kcal or Cal) is 1,000 calories.

⚙ Work is the transfer of energy that occurs when a force moves an object. The work done is the amount of energy (in J) gained by the object.

⚙ The work rate (the rate at which energy is changed from one energy store to another) is known as the power.

⚙ The power of a machine is the amount of work it does divided by the length of time it takes to do it:

$$\text{power} = \frac{\text{work done (w)}}{\text{time (t)}}$$

⚙ A transducer is a device that converts electricity into different energy stores – such as sound, light or motion – or vice versa. A loudspeaker is an example of a transducer.

▶ *A wind turbine converts the kinetic (movement) energy of the wind into electrical energy.*

DID YOU KNOW?
Wind turbines can generate electrical power from wind speeds as low as 5 km/h.

Heat and temperature

⚙ Heat is the transfer or movement of thermal energy from a region of higher temperature to a region of lower temperature. Thermal energy is the combined energy of moving molecules.

⚙ Temperature is a measure of the average kinetic (movement) energy of the molecules within a substance. Common units of measurement for temperature include degrees Celsius (°C) and Fahrenheit (°F).

⚙ Celsius is also known as centigrade, because water boils at 100°C, and 'cent' is the Latin prefix for '100'. Water freezes at 0°C. On the Fahrenheit scale, water boils at 212°F and freezes at 32°F.

⚙ The coldest temperature possible is absolute zero, or –273.15°C. At this temperature, molecules stop moving.

⚙ When you heat a substance, its temperature rises because heat makes its molecules move or vibrate faster. The same amount of heat will raise the temperatures of different substances by different amounts.

▲ *Water boils – turns from its liquid state into a gas – when heated to 100°C.*

▶ *In this globe, sea surface temperature is indicated by colour, from the coldest waters (black) through blue, purple and red to the hottest, yellow.*

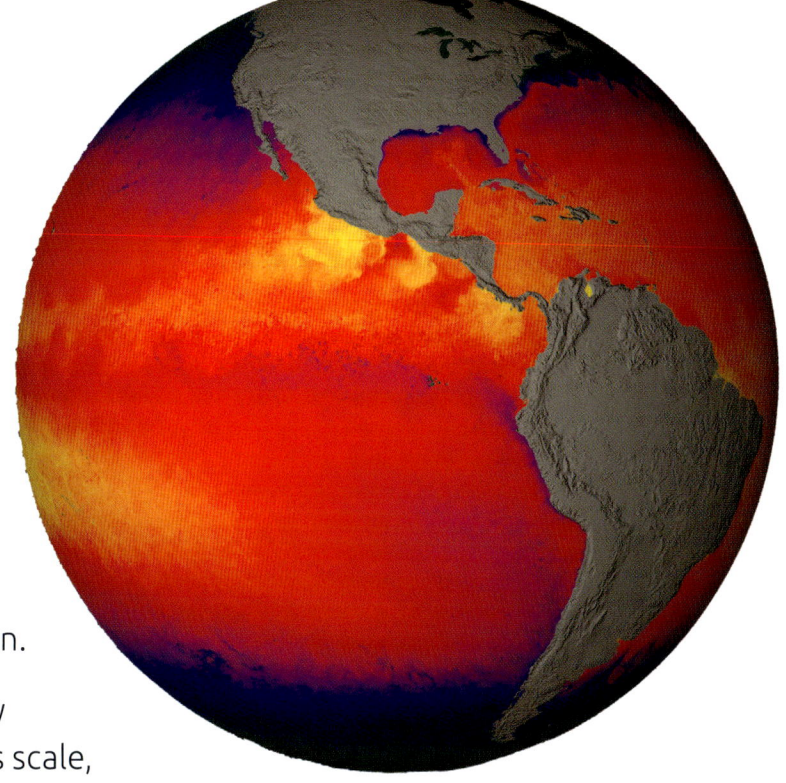

⚙ Heat spreads out from its origin, or source. It heats up its surroundings while the source of the heat cools down.

⚙ The Kelvin (K) scale is used by scientists. It is like the Celsius scale, but it begins at –273.15°C. This means that 0°C is equivalent to 273.15 K.

⚙ A log fire burns at a temperature of around 800°C. Molten magma is around 1,200°C. The surface of the Sun is around 6,000°C, while Earth's core is over 7,000°C. A lightning flash can reach 30,000°C.

⚙ The blood temperature of the human body is normally around 37°C. Body temperature above 40°C is very hot, and below 31°C is very cold. Anything hotter than 45°C hurts if it touches your skin, although some people can walk barefoot on burning coals as hot as 800°C.

⚙ When you hold your hand over a heater, you feel warmth because your hand absorbs the infrared radiation emitted (sent out) by the heater. This is a form of heat transfer that doesn't require a material medium (a substance made up of particles) to travel through. This is also how the Sun transmits heat to our planet through the vacuum of space.

Friction

⚙ Friction is a force that acts to oppose and restrict the motion of two surfaces that are in contact with each other.

⚙ The type of friction that prevents things from sliding is known as static friction.

⚙ The type that opposes and slows the motion of an object that is sliding is called dynamic friction.

⚙ Adhesive friction is a type of friction caused by the formation of temporary bonds between the surfaces of two objects in contact, which must be broken for motion to occur.

⚙ Fluid friction occurs between two fluids, or between a fluid and a solid. Fluid friction makes thick fluids 'viscous' (flowing less easily).

⚙ The harder two surfaces press together, the greater the force needed to overcome the friction.

▼ *Ice-bikes need grippy, sharp metal spikes on their tyres to make up for the lack of friction on the slippery ice.*

⚙ A smooth surface will have lower friction than a rough surface. This is because friction is the result of one object momentarily sticking to another object when the textures of their surfaces catch and rub against each other – a little like velcro.

DID YOU KNOW?
When two objects rub together they can transfer electrons, creating an electric charge called triboelectricity. This is where 'static' electricity comes from.

⚙ Friction often makes things hot. As the sliding surfaces are forced to slow, some of the energy of momentum (kinetic energy) is transferred into thermal energy.

⚙ Friction can generate enough heat to start a fire. Being able to start friction fires, using basic tools, is a very useful camping skill.

⚙ Oil reduces friction by creating a film that keeps solid surfaces apart.

⚙ Brakes are mechanisms that use dynamic friction to slow things down, such as the wheels of a bicycle.

⚙ Drag is friction between an object and a fluid substance – such as air or water – that it is moving through. It resists and slows a fast car, for example, or any aircraft moving through the air.

⚙ When we want to increase the friction of an object, we can add texture to its surface. Putting grooved soles on shoes or adding rough, non-slip tape to wooden stairs are both examples of this.

⚙ Machines use friction to generate 'traction'. For example, a car's tyres have deep ridges called treads. The treads use adhesive friction to help the vehicle to grip on to the road, which supports steering, acceleration and breaking. Treads also displace (push aside) water to increase the tyres' grip on wet road surfaces.

Thermodynamics

⚙ Energy cannot be destroyed, but it can be transformed into other energy stores – such as light and thermal energy.

⚙ Heat is the transfer or movement of thermal energy from a region of higher temperature to a region of lower temperature.

⚙ In a machine or mechanical system, some energy can be wasted, or 'dissipated', in the form of heat. A good example of this is the warming of a machine or an appliance's electrical cables when it is doing its work.

⚙ Scientists use the word 'entropy' to describe how much energy has become wasted or unusable. The less energy there is available for doing work, the greater the entropy.

⚙ German physicist Rudolf Clausius introduced the word 'entropy', in 1865, as a way to describe how everything happens because energy naturally moves from hot, high-energy areas to cold, low-energy areas.

⚙ Energy flows from hot regions to cold regions until both are equal in temperature (see page 70). Once this 'equilibrium' has been reached, there is no longer any energy difference for making things happen. So, entropy is said to be at a maximum.

⚙ Rudolf Clausius summed up this idea in the 1860s using two laws of thermodynamics.

⚙ The first law of thermodynamics says that the total energy in the Universe was fixed for ever at the beginning of time.

⚙ The second law of thermodynamics states that all energy differences tend to 'even out' over time, so the entropy must always increase.

▼ *Electrical cables may feel warm due to heat dissipation.*

◄ *Friction is used to generate heat and ignite the phosphorus at the tip of these matches. The fire then uses the stored energy in the wood to fuel itself, expelling energy in the form of heat and light. Once the fuel is used up, it cannot be used again.*

Engines

⚙ Engines are machines that convert fuel into movement. Most work by burning fuel to create gases that expand rapidly as they get hot.

⚙ Engines that burn fuel to generate power are called 'heat engines'. The burning process is called 'combustion'. Internal combustion engines, such as those in cars and jets, burn fuel on the inside.

⚙ In car and diesel train engines, hot gases swell up inside a 'combustion chamber' and push against a piston or turbine.

⚙ External combustion engines, such as those in steam engines, burn fuel on the outside – in a separate boiler that creates hot steam to drive a piston or turbine.

⚙ Although the use of electric and 'hybrid' vehicles is on the rise, petrol and diesel remain the most common fuels for motor vehicles. However, reserves of these are limited. Some engines now burn biofuels, such as ethanol and methanol, which are made from plants such as maize.

▼ *In a turbofan engine, cold air mixes with hot gases to produce thrust.*

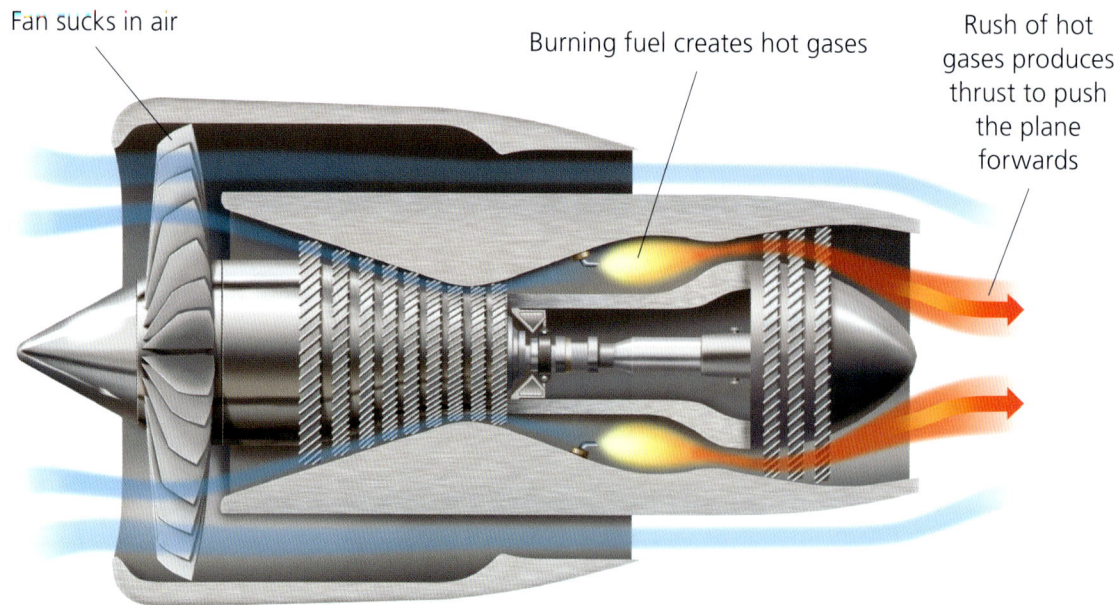

Fan sucks in air

Burning fuel creates hot gases

Rush of hot gases produces thrust to push the plane forwards

⚙ Petrol, diesel and biofuels create gases that pollute the air, so some engines now use hydrogen. Electric cars use a battery that is converted into power by an electrical motor, rather than an engine.

⚙ Engines with pistons that go back and forth inside cylinders are called reciprocating engines.

⚙ In four-stroke engines (used in most cars), the pistons go up and down – four times – every time they are thrust down by the hot gases. In two-stroke engines (used in small motorcycles and lawn mowers), a piston is pushed by the hot gases every time it moves down.

⚙ In jets and rockets, the hot gases rapidly expand to create an equal and opposing force, known as thrust.

⚙ In these jet engines (see below and left), air is taken in at the front, compressed by fans, then sprayed with fuel and set alight. The burning gases expand, blast past more fans (the turbine) and rush out through the back of the engine – creating thrust to power the plane forwards.

▼ *In a turboprop engine, hot gases from a jet engine drive a turbine, which rotates a shaft connected to the propeller.*

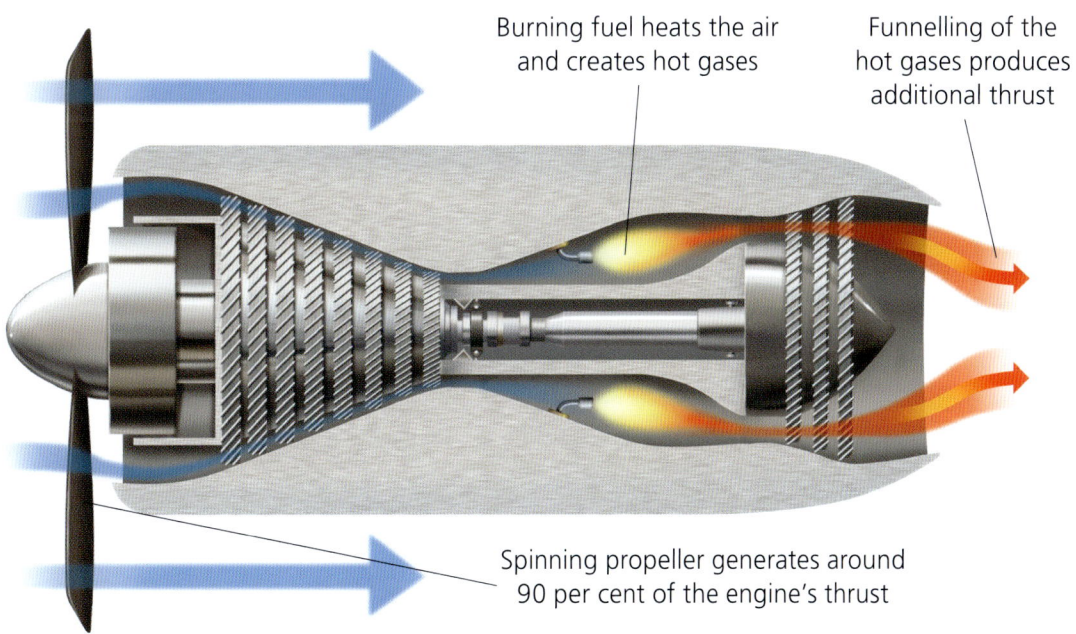

Burning fuel heats the air and creates hot gases

Funnelling of the hot gases produces additional thrust

Spinning propeller generates around 90 per cent of the engine's thrust

77

Electricity

⚙ Electricity is a form of energy transfer that makes use of the movement of charged particles – electrons in particular (see pages 8–9). It is the major source of power for much of the world.

⚙ All atoms carry a tiny electrical charge. This is a force, which either pulls bits of atoms together (attracts them) or pushes them apart (repels them). Two particles with the same charge repel each other, while two particles with opposing charges attract one another.

⚙ Atoms contain protons, neutrons and electrons. Electrons carry a negative charge, while protons have a positive charge. Most atoms have equal numbers of positive and negative particles, so they usually carry a 'balanced' electrical charge.

⚙ The movement of electrons can produce an electric current – a flow of electricity. A material through which electrons can flow, such as copper, is called a 'conductor'. Materials that stop electrons passing through, such as rubber, are called 'insulators'.

⚙ Static electricity is the build-up of electrical charge on an insulator. It is the result of electrons being shifted to the insulator by friction. This is why rubbing a balloon against a woolly jumper creates static.

▼ *During a thunderstorm, a negative electrical charge builds up at the base of a cloud, while the ground has a positive charge. A spark or 'bolt' of lightning jumps between them to release the charge.*

Electric circuits

⚙ An electric circuit is an unbroken loop of conducting material along which an electrical charge may flow.

⚙ There are three basic components in an electric circuit: a conductor, an energy source and an object for the circuit to power.

⚙ A current will only flow if there is an energy source, such as a cell or a battery (a collection of connected cells), to provide an electromotive force (EMF).

⚙ An EMF is created by a battery or generator. Without an EMF, charged electrons will just move randomly inside the conductor in different directions. Random movement does not produce an electric current.

⚙ When a conductor is connected to a battery, the negatively charged electrons are attracted to the battery's positive terminal, so they flow towards it in one direction. This flow creates an electric current.

⚙ Batteries give electrical, potential energy to the electrons. The amount of electrical energy varies at different points in a circuit. This difference, known as the potential difference, is measured in volts (V).

⚙ The rate at which current flows is measured in amperes, or amps. It depends on the voltage and the resistance (how much the circuit obstructs the flow of current). Resistance is measured in ohms.

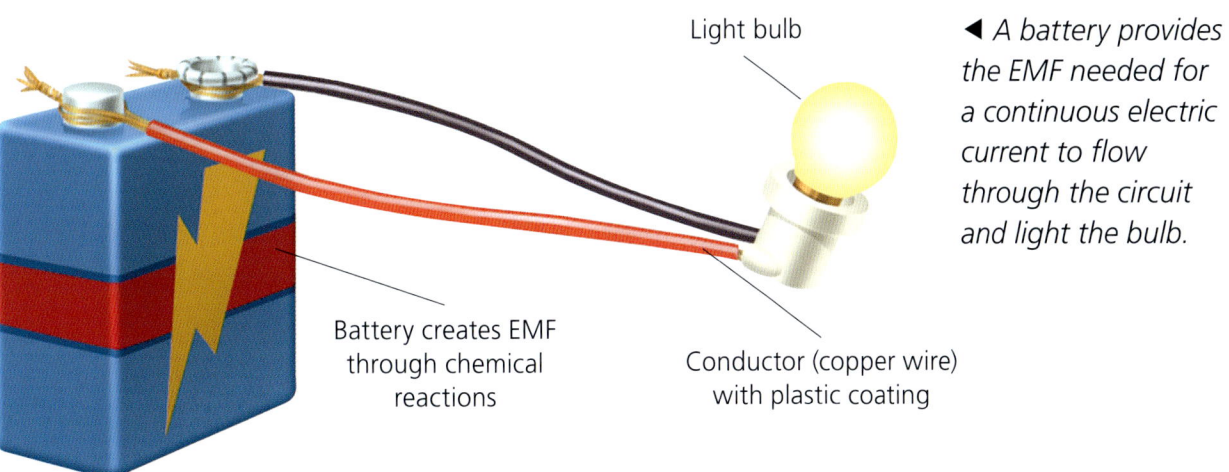

Light bulb

◀ *A battery provides the EMF needed for a continuous electric current to flow through the circuit and light the bulb.*

Battery creates EMF through chemical reactions

Conductor (copper wire) with plastic coating

Magnetism

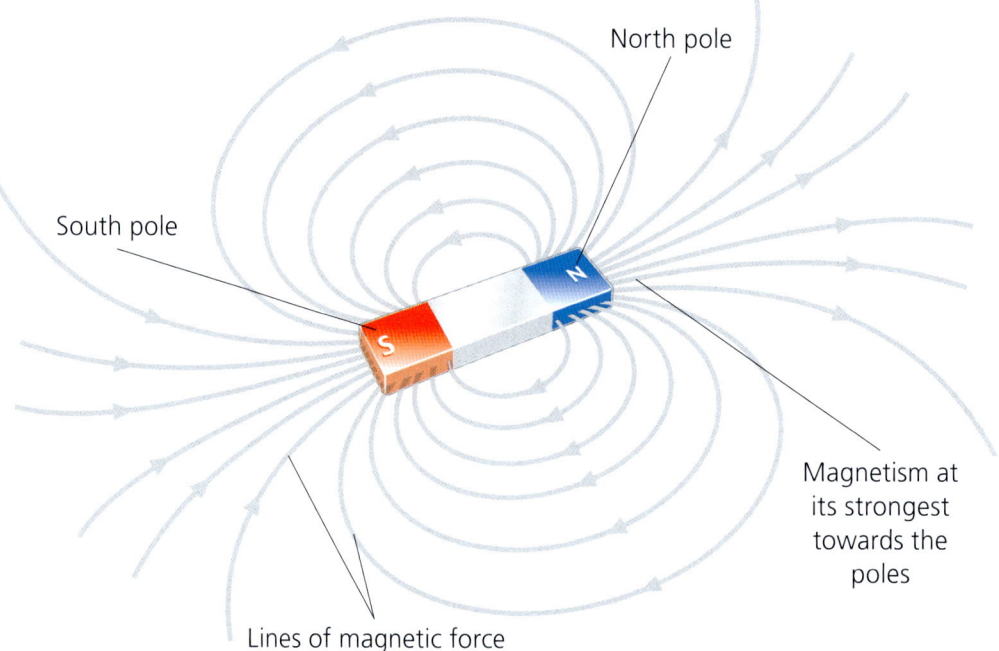

North pole

South pole

Magnetism at its strongest towards the poles

Lines of magnetic force

▲ *A bar magnet is made from a 'ferromagnetic' material such as iron or steel. Its lines of magnetic force originate from the north pole and curve around to the south pole, forming continuous loops.*

⚙ Magnetism is the property of some materials to attract or repel 'like' materials. A magnet is a material that has this property.

⚙ A magnetic field is the region, around a magnet, in which its magnetic force can be detected. An electric current creates a magnetic field.

⚙ A magnet has north and south 'poles' near each end. The magnetic field is strongest at the poles. 'Like' poles (for example, north poles of two magnets) repel each other, and 'unlike' poles attract each other.

⚙ Earth has a magnetic field created by electric currents inside its iron core. The magnetic north pole is close to the geographic North Pole.

⚙ If suspended freely, a magnet will turn so that its north pole points towards Earth's geographic North Pole (which is actually the planet's magnetic south pole – hence the attraction of north to south).

⚙ The strength of a magnet is measured in teslas. The Earth's magnetic field is approximately 0.00005 teslas.

Electromagnetism

- Electromagnetism is the combination of electricity and magnetism. Every electric current creates its own magnetic field.

- An electromagnet is a strong magnet that is only magnetic when an electric current passes through it. It is made by wrapping a coil of wire (a solenoid) around a core of iron.

- Electromagnets are used in many electric machines, from ticket machines and loudspeakers to telephones, motors and generators.

- Magnetic levitation (or Maglev) trains use electromagnets to support the train above the rails through magnetic repulsion.

- When an electric wire is moved across a magnetic field, a current is created, or 'induced', in the wire. This is the basis of every method of generating electricity.

- Unlike permanent magnets, electromagnets can be switched on and off by controlling the flow of electric current.

- 'Electromagnetic field' describes the area around an electric or magnetic object in which the electromagnetic force is effective.

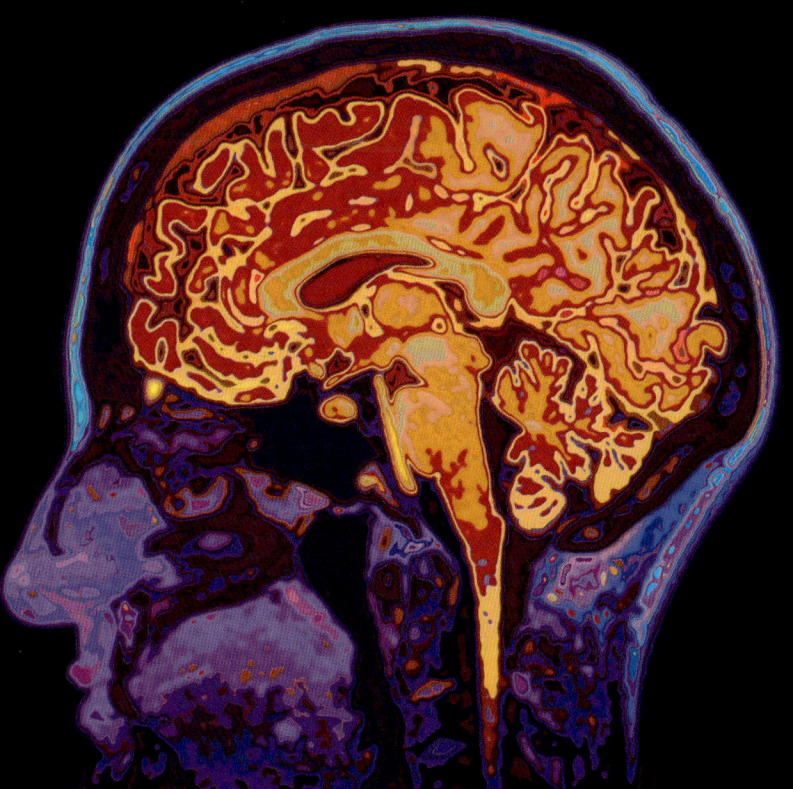

◄ *Magnetic Resonance Imaging (MRI) is a scanning procedure that uses strong magnetic fields and radio waves to create detailed images of areas inside the body, such as the brain.*

81

Electromagnetic spectrum

⚙ Electromagnetic radiation is energy emitted by atoms. It travels in minute packets of energy, called 'photons', that can behave either as particles or as waves.

⚙ Waves of electromagnetic radiation can vary in length and frequency. The electromagnetic spectrum is the full range or radiation types.

⚙ The longest radiation waves are more than 100 km in length, while the shortest are less than a billionth of a millimetre long.

⚙ The human eye can see just a small range of wavelengths, known as visible light (right). Every colour we see has its own wavelength.

⚙ Infrared (IR) is light given off by warm objects in waves that are too long for the human eye to detect (see page 71. Ultraviolet (UV) is light given off by very hot objects in waves that are too short for the eye to detect.

⚙ Waves that are longer than visible light include microwaves (used in microwave ovens) and radio waves (used by radios, TV broadcasts, mobile phones and wireless networks).

▶ *The electromagnetic spectrum ranges from long-wavelength, low-energy radio waves to short-wavelength, high-energy gamma rays.*

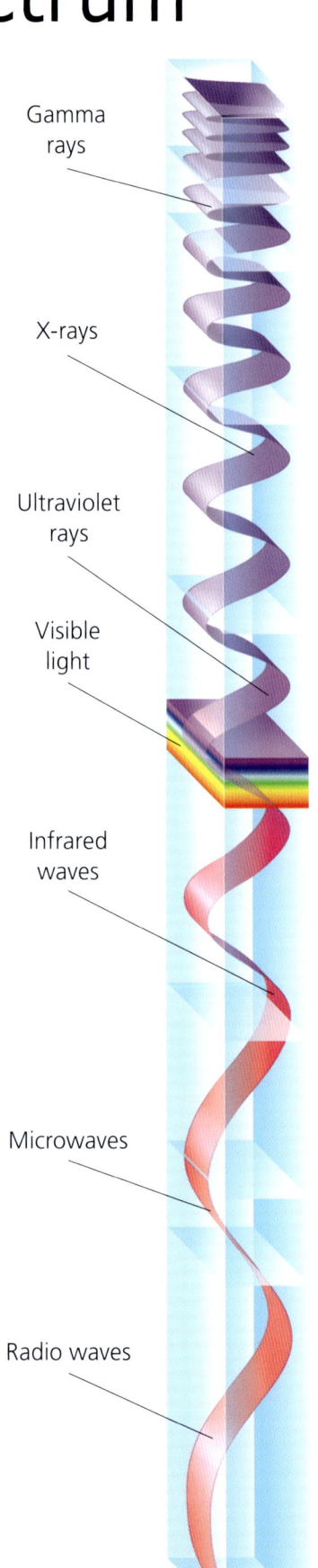

Gamma rays

X-rays

Ultraviolet rays

Visible light

Infrared waves

Microwaves

Radio waves

▲ *All objects and animals emit infrared waves. By measuring these waves, using an infrared camera, we can create a 'temperature map' that indicates hot and cool spots. Hot spots show up in shades of red, while cool spots are displayed in shades of blue.*

⚙ Waves that are shorter than visible light – such as UV, X-rays and gamma rays – are very energetic, and can penetrate (pass through) some solid materials that block light, including people. This means it can be harmful to be exposed to them.

⚙ In small doses, the UV in sunlight may create a 'suntan' on skin, but in large doses it can cause skin cancer.

⚙ X-rays are harmless in brief doses – and their waves are short enough to pass through most body tissues, except bone. This is why they can be used to create medical X-ray photos.

⚙ Gamma rays are dangerous even in small doses. However, they can be used safely in some body scans, and to 'irradiate' seeds to prevent them from growing until they are needed.

Electronics

⚙ Electronics is the technology of electrical control systems, at the heart of everything from mobile phones to personal computers (PCs).

⚙ Electronic components control operations by switching tiny electrical circuits on and off.

⚙ Transistors are the key components of every electronic system. They control the flow of electricity.

⚙ A transistor controls currents automatically because it is made from a material called a semiconductor, which can have its electrical conductivity altered by a small voltage or current.

⚙ Diodes are transistors with two connection points: an 'in' and an 'out'. They are simple switches, turning the current on or off.

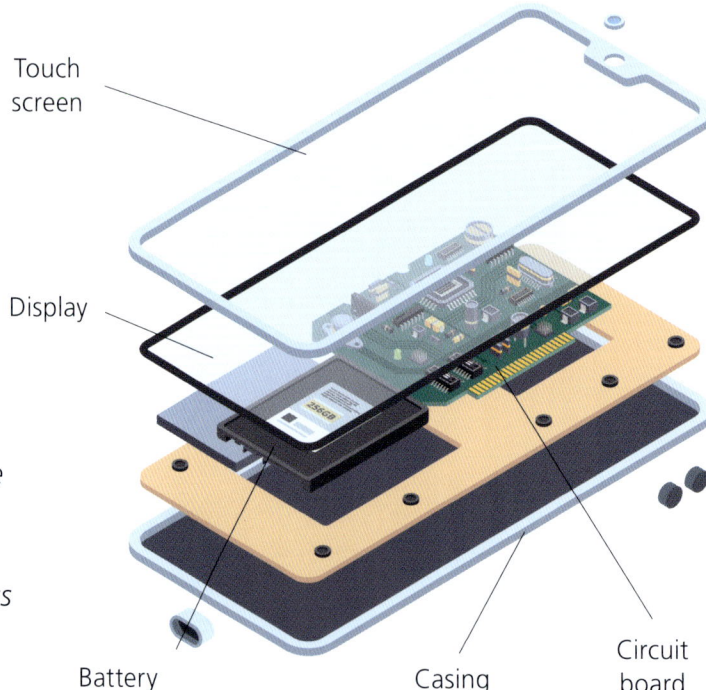

Touch screen

Display

▶ *Mobile phones were made possible by the invention of the silicon chip. Inside the phone, a chip translates speech into a digital form suitable for wireless transmission to the nearest phone mast.*

Battery

Casing

Circuit board

▲ *Circuit boards are made from insulating materials such as resin, coated with a layer of copper foil. The foil is etched into the board to create electronic circuits. This reduces the number of wires and cables that have to fit into an electronic device, allowing modern computers to be much smaller and more efficient.*

⚙ Triodes are transistors with three connection points: an 'in', an 'out' and a 'control'. They can amplify the current or reduce it.

⚙ A silicon chip consists of thousands of transistors linked by thin metal strips, integrated (contained) within a single crystal (chip) of silicon, which is a semiconductor.

Radiation

⚙ Radiation is a way for 'unstable', radioactive atoms to get rid of excess energy. Electromagnetic radiation is energy that travels as photons at the speed of light. Particulate radiation is the emission of subatomic particles such as alpha particles, beta particles and neutrons.

⚙ Particulate radiation includes cosmic rays (streams of particles from the stars) and 'radioactivity' that occurs when unstable atoms degrade (break down) in order to become stable.

⚙ Radiation can be harmful. It can damage and kill human, animal and plant cells.

⚙ Bacteria can survive a dose of radiation many thousands of times stronger than a dose that might kill a person.

⚙ The radiation released by radioactivity is commonly measured in becquerels (Bq). The radiation dose a person receives is measured in roentgens (rads) or in grays (Gy). 100 rads is equal to 1 Gy.

⚙ An X-ray scan exposes the human body to a relatively small amount of radiation, equivalent to a few days of natural 'background' radiation.

▼ *People who are exposed to high levels of radiation, such as nuclear scientists, often wear personal radiation dosimeters to measure the amount of radiation to which they are being exposed as they carry out their work.*

▲ *The fuel burned in nuclear power stations becomes highly radioactive when 'spent' (after being used) and must be disposed of safely. Nuclear technicians use a variety of machines and methods to avoid handling radioactive waste directly.*

⚙ A dose of 400 rad would give you extreme radiation sickness and, if left untreated, would be fatal in a matter of days. Even when treated, such a dose would have lasting negative effects on the body.

⚙ In 1986, an accident at the Chernobyl nuclear power station in a region of the Soviet Union (now Ukraine) released large amounts of radiation into the atmosphere, resulting in many deaths and the contamination of millions of acres of land.

⚙ Brazil nuts are naturally radioactive, because their extensive root systems absorb radium (a radioactive metal) from the soil. Their level of radioactivity is safe – comparable to natural background radiation.

Light and atoms

⚙ Atoms give out light after they have gained energy. They take on this energy – very briefly – by absorbing photons of light or other electromagnetic waves, or when hit by other particles.

⚙ Normally, atoms are in a 'ground' state in which their electrons circle close to the nucleus (see page 8), where their energy is at its weakest.

⚙ When an atom absorbs a photon containing energy, an electron moves to a higher, unstable, 'excited' state – further away from the nucleus.

⚙ An atom only stays excited for a fraction of a second before the electron 'relaxes' back to a lower, more stable energy level – closer to the nucleus.

⚙ To return to this more stable level, the electron releases the excess energy it gained as a photon, a packet of electromagnetic radiation (see page 82).

◀ *Astronomers use a process called 'spectroscopy' to tell what distant stars are made of. It works by analysing the colours in the light emitted by their atoms.*

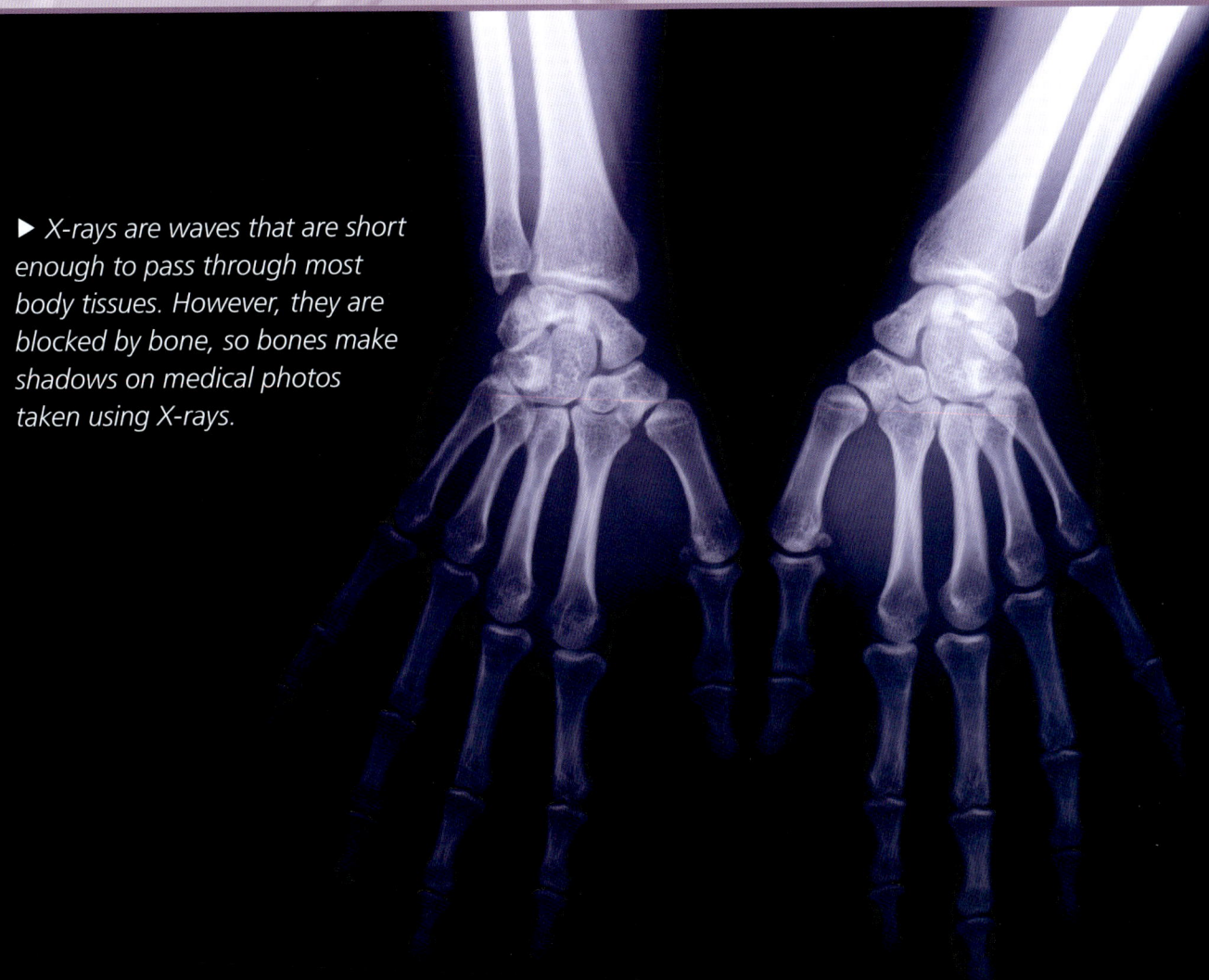

▶ *X-rays are waves that are short enough to pass through most body tissues. However, they are blocked by bone, so bones make shadows on medical photos taken using X-rays.*

⚙ An electron's 'relaxation' to the lower energy level is controlled by the specific amount of energy in the emitted photon. Larger emissions send out higher-energy, short-wave photons such as X-rays.

⚙ The colour of the light that an atom sends out also depends on the size of the energy emission created as its electrons relax.

⚙ Each type of atom has its own range of electron energy emissions. As a result, each sends out a unique 'fingerprint' of colours from light's visible spectrum.

⚙ The range of colours that each kind of atom sends out is known as its emission spectrum.

Visible light

⚙ When we refer to 'light' we usually mean visible light, which is the only form of electromagnetic radiation that we can see.

⚙ During the day, light appears to be all around us, but only a few things are actually sources of light. Natural light sources include stars, such as our Sun. Artificial sources include battery-operated and electric lights.

⚙ Most objects are visible to us because they reflect the light that is produced by light sources. If something is not a light source and does not reflect light, we cannot see it.

⚙ Light travels in straight lines, known as rays. Light rays change direction if they are reflected off or pass through an object or substance, but they still remain straight.

⚙ If the path of a light ray is blocked, a shadow forms.

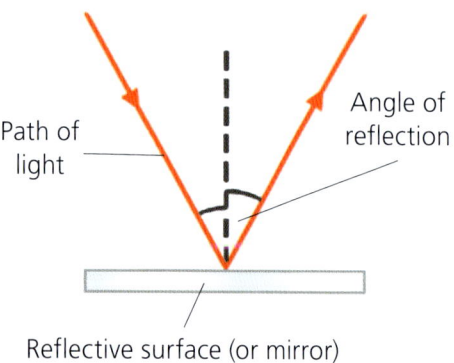

Path of light

Angle of reflection

Reflective surface (or mirror)

◀ ▼ *When looking into a flat mirror, we see light rays reflected, all together, at the same angle in which they arrived, so they present an accurate image (left). A mirror that isn't flat reflects them at different angles, distorting the image (below).*

Light sources

⚙ The main source of natural light on Earth is the Sun. The hot gases on its surface glow fiercely, radiating light in all directions.

⚙ The brightness (or 'luminous intensity') of a light source is measured in candelas (Cd), with 1 Cd having about the same luminous intensity as a small candle.

⚙ The Sun's surface pumps out 23 billion Cd per m². Laser lights are even brighter, but very small.

⚙ The amount of light falling on a surface is measured in lux, with 1 lux equal to the amount of light from a source of 1 Cd, from 1 m away. You'll need around 500 lux to read the words in this book!

⚙ Some electric light bulbs are 'incandescent', which means that their light comes from a thin tungsten wire, or filament, that glows when heated by an electric current.

⚙ English physicist and chemist Sir Joseph Swan and American inventors Thomas Edison and Hiram Maxim all invented incandescent light bulbs, independently of each other, in around 1878–79.

⚙ A fluorescent light has a glass tube coated on the inside with powders called phosphors. Electricity causes the gases inside the tube to send out UV rays, which hit the phosphors, making them fluoresce (glow).

⚙ In a neon light, a high electric current makes the gas inside the tube electrically charged, causing it to glow.

◄ *This low-energy light bulb uses a glowing gas to emit light, instead of a glowing filament of wire (as in an incandescent bulb).*

Colour

⚙ Colour is the way our eyes and brain detect different wavelengths of light.

⚙ We see the longest light waves as the colour red. Waves that appear red are about 700 nanometres (nm) in length (1 nm = 1 billionth of a metre).

⚙ The shortest light waves – of around 380 nm in length – are seen by human eyes as the colour violet.

⚙ Some light, such as sunlight and the light from ordinary light bulbs, is known as white light – but it is actually a mixture of every colour.

⚙ The world around us appears to us in different colours because molecules in different surfaces reflect and absorb particular wavelengths of light.

⚙ 'Iridescence' is the effect we see as a shimmering rainbow of colours that flashes across surfaces such as peacock feathers, butterfly wings and compact discs (CDs).

⚙ Iridescence can be caused by the way a surface scatters the light hitting it into colours. It can also be caused by interference, which occurs when an object has a thin, transparent surface layer that refracts (bends) light.

◄ The shimmering blue of this butterfly is iridescence created by tiny air pockets in the scales on its wings.

Mixing colours

▶ *Each circle is a primary colour of light (red, green and blue). Where two of them overlap, you see the subtractive primaries (magenta, cyan and yellow).*

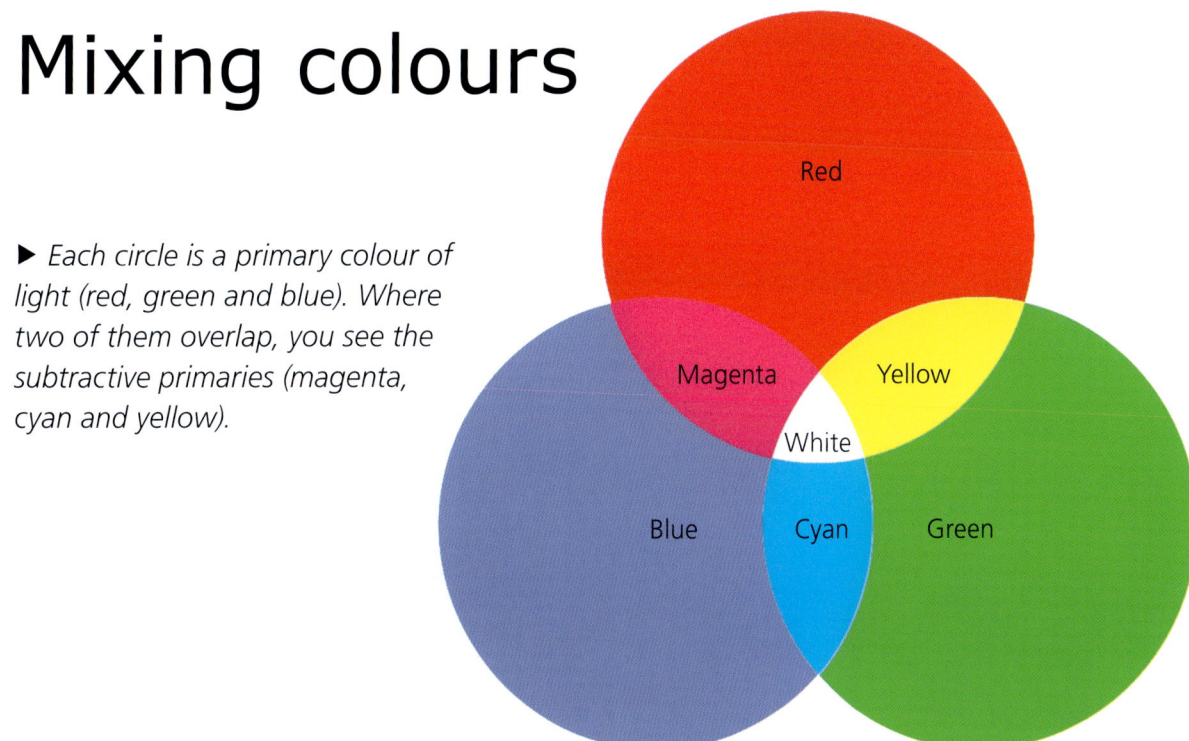

⚙ There are three primary colours of light – red, green and blue. They can be mixed to make any other colour by varying their proportions.

⚙ The primary colours of light are called 'additive' primaries, because they can be added together to make other colours. Each additive primary is one-third of the spectrum of white light, so combining them creates white (see above).

⚙ When two additive primaries are added together, they make a third colour known as a 'subtractive' primary.

⚙ The three subtractive primaries are magenta (red plus blue), cyan (blue plus green) and yellow (green plus red). They, too, can be mixed in various proportions to make other colours.

⚙ Surfaces appear as certain colours to human eyes because they soak up certain colours of white light and reflect the others. The colour the eye perceives is a combination of the colours being reflected.

⚙ We see the colour black when all light wavelengths have been absorbed by a surface. This occurs when the object is a combination of colours that, together, absorb the entire spectrum of visible light.

Spectrum

⚙ A spectrum is a range of different wavelengths of electromagnetic radiation.

⚙ The 'white' light of sunlight can be broken up into its spectrum of colours using a triangular prism of glass or acrylic (hard plastic).

⚙ When a prism is lit by a beam of white light, it refracts short wavelengths of the light more than longer ones. This causes the light to split into bands ranging from violet (the shortest wavelength) to red (the longest).

⚙ The order of colours in a spectrum always begins with red, followed by orange, yellow, green, blue, indigo and violet. You can remember the order by imagining a character called 'ROY G. BIV': each letter in the name stands for a colour of the visible spectrum.

▶ *In a darkened room, a narrow beam of white light is split into a spectrum – by refraction – as it passes through a prism.*

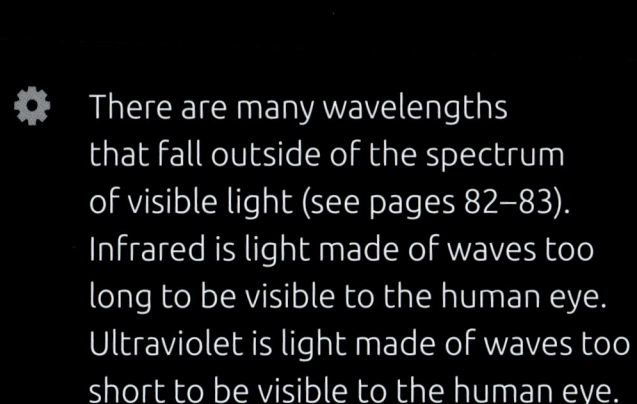

⚙ There are many wavelengths that fall outside of the spectrum of visible light (see pages 82–83). Infrared is light made of waves too long to be visible to the human eye. Ultraviolet is light made of waves too short to be visible to the human eye.

⚙ Spectral analysis is the study of the spectrum created when a solid, liquid or gas glows.

⚙ Every substance produces its own unique spectrum, so spectral analysis can help to identify individual substances.

DID YOU KNOW?
Spectral analysis can reveal what anything, from a distant galaxy to a drug, is composed of.

Sound

⚙ Most sounds you hear, from the whisper of the wind to the roar of a jet, are actually vibrations in the form of pressure waves.

⚙ Every sound originates with something vibrating, such as the strings of a guitar twanging to and fro. This makes particles in the air vibrate, too, and it is these vibrations that carry sounds to your ears.

⚙ The vibrations that carry sound through a material – such as the air – are called sound waves, and they move by alternately squeezing a material's molecules together and then spreading them apart.

⚙ The parts of the air that are squeezed are called condensations, while the parts that are stretched are called rarefactions.

⚙ Sound waves travel faster through liquids and solids, because the molecules in liquids and solids are more closely packed together than they are in gases such as air.

⚙ There is complete silence in a vacuum (a space that does not contain any matter) because there are no molecules for carrying sound.

◀ A speaker converts electrical signals into corresponding patterns of sound waves.

Atomic bomb: 210–280 dB

⚙ Sound travels at around 344 m/sec in air at 20°C, but 386 m/sec in air at 100°C. It travels at approximately 1,500 m/sec in water and about 6,000 m/sec in steel.

⚙ The speed of sound is around a million times slower than light. This is why, during a thunderstorm, you see a flash of lightning before you hear the thunder.

Jet take-off: 140 dB

⚙ The loudness (volume) of a sound is usually measured in decibels (dB). A decibel is one-tenth of a bel, the unit of sound named after Scottish-born, American inventor Alexander Graham Bell.

⚙ An increase of 10 points on the decibel scale means that a sound has become ten times louder.

Thunder: 100 dB

⚙ The quietest sound audible to human ears is 0 dB, and we can only hear a change in a sound's volume if it is of 1 dB or more.

⚙ A rustle of leaves or a quiet whisper is 10 dB. Quiet talking is 30–40 dB, and loud talking is about 60 dB.

City street: 70 dB

⚙ The noise level on a city street is about 70 dB. Thunder is approximately 100 dB, while the loudest screams ever recorded were around 130 dB. A jet taking off is 110–140 dB. The loudest sound ever made by human technology was the detonation of an atomic bomb, at more than 210 dB.

Talking: 40 dB

⚙ The amount of energy in a sound is measured in watts per square metre (W/m²). A sound of 0 dB is a thousand billionth (or one-trillionth) of 1 W/m².

▶ *A range of different sounds on the decibel (dB) scale.*

Rustling leaves: 10 dB

Echoes and acoustics

⚙ An echo is a reflection of sound – bouncing off of an object or surface – that is heard slightly after the initial, direct sound.

⚙ Our ears can hear an echo only if it comes back more than 0.1 seconds after the original sound. In 0.1 seconds, sound travels 34 m, so we can only hear echoes that are reflected back from at least 17 m away.

⚙ Smooth, hard surfaces provide the best echoes, because they cause a minimum amount of disruption to the reflecting sound waves.

▼ *Hunting whales, such as the beluga (below), send out sonic clicks. These pulses bounce back as echoes to give the whales information about the position of any objects that might be nearby – such as the food they are hunting for.*

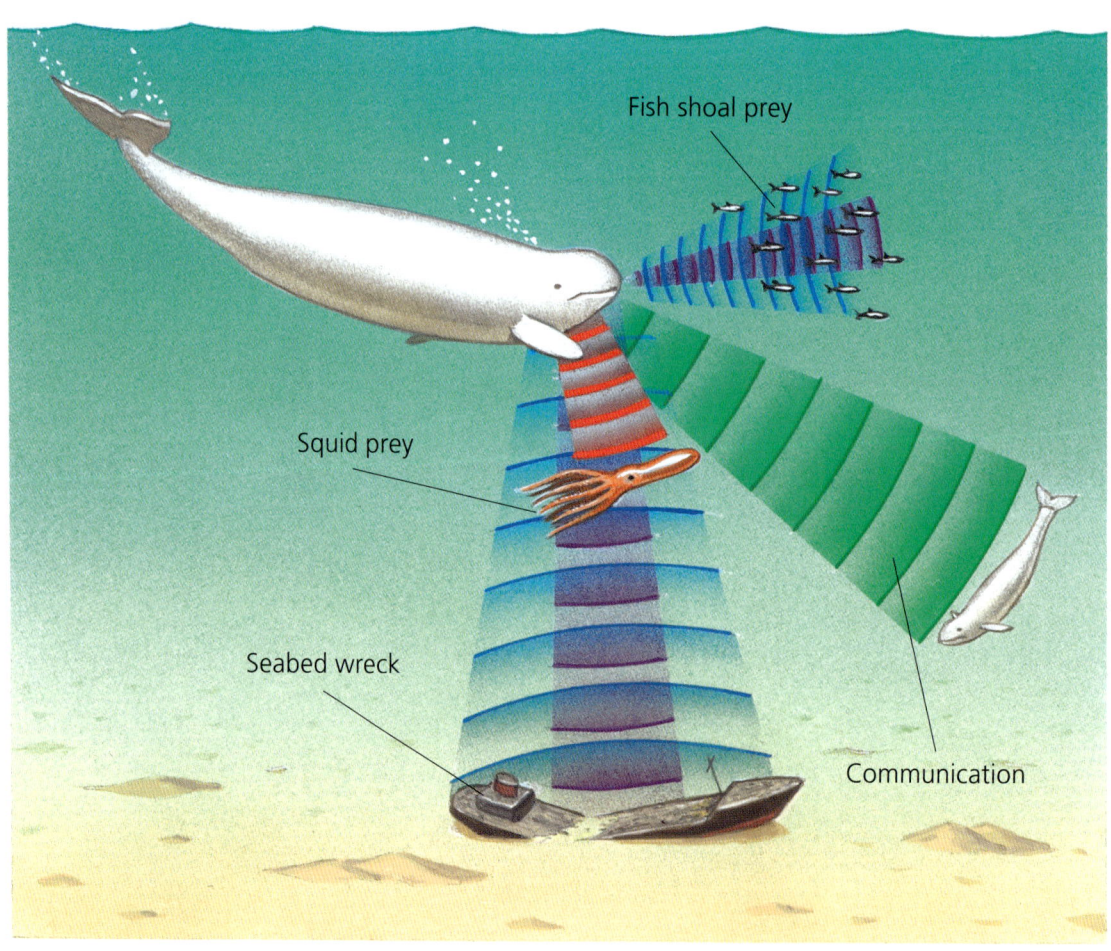

Fish shoal prey

Squid prey

Seabed wreck

Communication

⚙ Acoustics is the study of how sounds are created, transmitted and received. It also refers to the sound properties of a building.

⚙ Concert halls are designed to use echoes effectively to project sound. If a concert hall has too much echo, the echoing sounds will interfere with new sounds. However, a complete absence of echoes results in a muffled, lifeless sound. Acoustic engineers try to find a balance.

⚙ The sound of live music can often be heard fading, even after the musicians have stopped playing. This delay is called the reverberation time. Concert halls typically have a reverberation time of 2 seconds. The hard, smooth interior of a cathedral, with high ceilings, may cause reverberations of up to 8 seconds, producing a less defined sound.

▲ *In 1969, acoustic engineers installed these distinctive 'mushroom' sound cushions to reduce echoes from the vast dome of the Royal Albert Hall in London, UK. This has improved the sound balance and quality of concerts performed at this famous venue.*

Musical sounds

⚙ Like all sounds, a musical note is created by vibrations of air. Musicians control the frequency and volume of these vibrations to play tunes.

⚙ The pitch (the 'high' or 'low' level) of a musical note depends upon the frequency of the vibrations.

⚙ Sound frequency is measured in hertz (Hz), which refers to the number of cycles or sound waves per second (1 Hz is one cycle per second).

⚙ Human ears can hear sounds within a frequency range of 20–20,000 Hz.

⚙ The middle C note on a piano measures 262 Hz. A modern, 88-key piano has a frequency range of 27.5–4,186 Hz.

⚙ The highest singing voice can reach the E above a piano's top C note (around 4,350 Hz), while the lowest note on a piano is about 27.5 Hz.

⚙ Few sounds have only one pitch. Most have a fundamental (low) pitch and higher 'overtones'.

⚙ The frequency at which an object naturally vibrates is called its resonant frequency. A musical note can shatter glass if its frequency matches the resonant frequency of the glass itself.

Mouthpiece

Standard saxophone has 23 finger-operated keys, pressed in different combinations to make musical notes

▶ *The shape of the saxophone controls the vibrations of air blown into it to create a musical sound.*

▶ *The sound of a violin is created by the regular vibrations of the strings as the bow is drawn across them.*

Time

⚙ Time is measured in seconds, minutes, hours, days, weeks, months and years. A clock is a device used to measure periods of time.

⚙ The science of how time is accurately measured is called chronometry. The study of clockmaking itself is called horology, and a person who makes clocks is known as a horologist.

⚙ Clocks are controlled by mechanisms with repeating motions. Ordinary clocks do not keep perfect time – they usually gain or lose at least a fraction of a second every day.

⚙ Since 1967, standard worldwide time has been set by 'atomic' clocks. The most precise atomic clocks – which use the vibrations of caesium or strontium atoms – lose less than a second over billions of years.

⚙ Atomic clocks are kept regular by the movement of certain atoms. Caesium atoms vibrate at a rate of 9,192,631,770 cycles per second, while strontium atoms are even faster (and therefore even more accurate), vibrating at 429,228,004,229,952 cycles per second.

⚙ The strontium atomic clocks at JILA, a scientific institute in Colorado, USA, are among the most accurate clocks on Earth. One of them could run for around 40 billion years without gaining or losing a second!

▶ *The idea of time zones began in the 1870s and '80s, as a way to standardise timekeeping for railway timetables. Air travel has made them even more important. The time within a certain time zone is the same everywhere, but the time is different in all of the other time zones.*

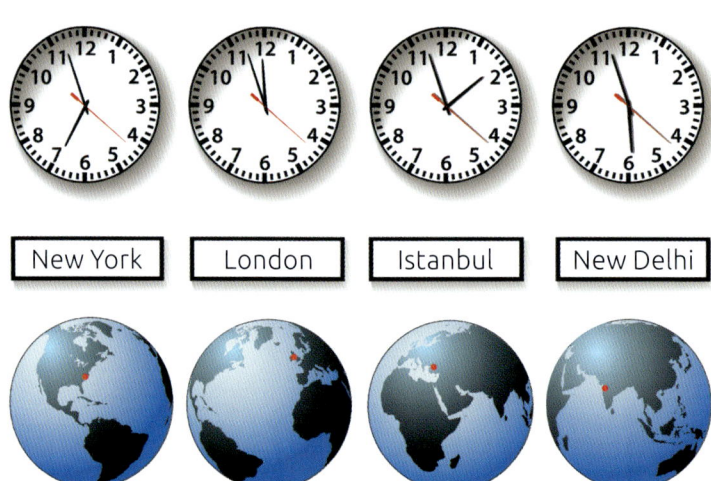

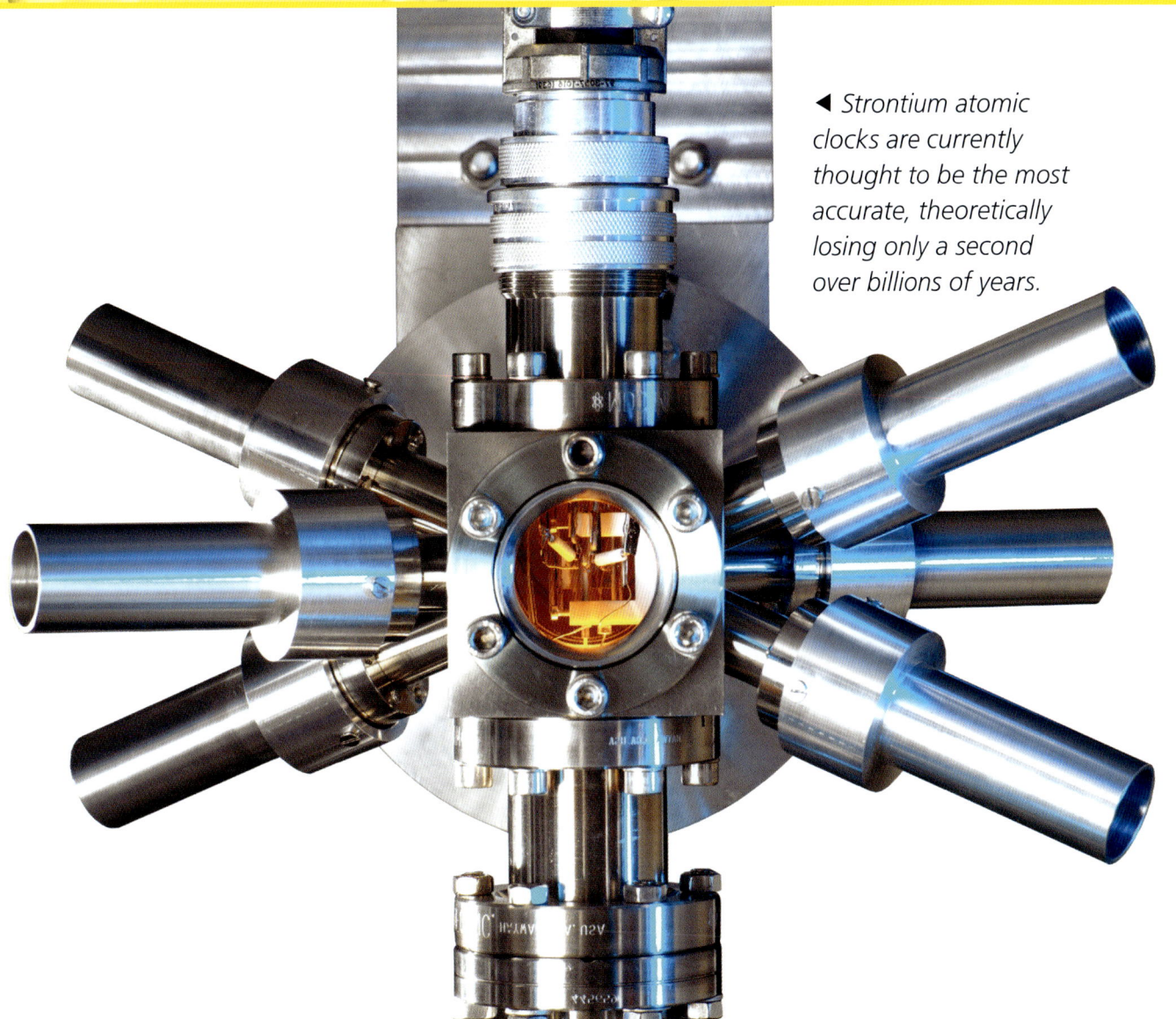

◀ *Strontium atomic clocks are currently thought to be the most accurate, theoretically losing only a second over billions of years.*

⚙ Some scientists think time is the fourth dimension (the other three being length, width and height). This suggests the theory that time could run in any direction.

⚙ Distant stars are so far away that their light can take many years to reach us. This means we see them as they were years ago, not as they are now. So, time actually varies according to where you are.

⚙ Albert Einstein's General Theory of Relativity (see page 104) shows us that time is affected by gravity, and runs slower nearer to strong gravitational fields such as those of stars. This is known to physicists as gravitational time dilation.

Relativity

▶ *Gravity is so intense around a black hole that it curves and warps space-time.*

⚙ Albert Einstein was a German-born theoretical physicist. He created two theories of 'relativity' that have revolutionised the way scientists think about the Universe. These are called the Special Theory of Relativity (1905) and the General Theory of Relativity (1915).

⚙ According to Einstein's theories, time is relative. It depends entirely on where you are and how you are moving when you measure it. Someone elsewhere will get a different measurement.

⚙ In his Special Theory of Relativity, Einstein showed that you cannot even measure speed relative to light, the fastest known thing in the Universe. This is because the speed of light is constant (unchanging): it doesn't depend on how fast the source of the light is moving – or the speed of someone looking at the light.

⚙ Einstein realised that the constant speed of light would result in some strange effects on other objects moving at very high speeds.

⚙ Einstein's General Theory of Relativity showed that gravity bends space-time, leading scientists to predict the existence of black holes. Black holes are not actually 'holes' – they are highly dense concentrations of matter in space, where gravity is so strong that even light is pulled into them.

⚙ A total eclipse of the Sun in 1919 gave English scientist Arthur Eddington the opportunity to observe the Sun's gravity bending light, proving Einstein's General Theory of Relativity is correct!

⚙ It wasn't until the 1960s that astronomers were able to observe the effects of relativity around super-dense objects such as black holes.

▶ *With his theories of relativity, Einstein overturned our previous understanding of the nature of time and space.*

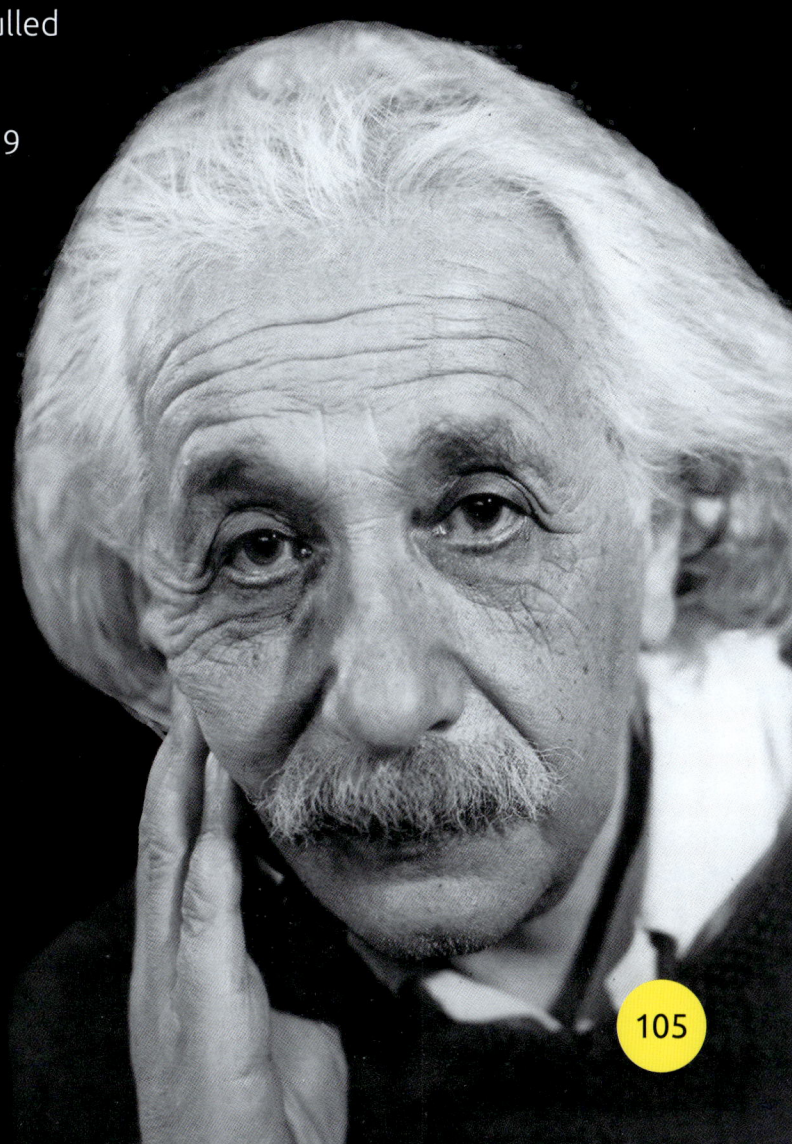

Quantum physics

⚙ In the 1890s, German physicist Max Planck showed that radiation from a hot object is not in the form of waves as everyone thought at the time. Instead it is emitted in fixed, tiny packets of energy called quanta (singular: quantum), which together behave like waves.

⚙ When light strikes certain atoms, it creates electricity in what is called the 'photoelectric' effect. Einstein realised that this can be explained if light travels in quanta, rather than in waves.

⚙ To Planck, quanta were just a mathematical idea. Einstein showed they were real. Light quanta later became known as photons (see page 82).

⚙ In 1913, Danish physicist Niels Bohr showed how the different energy levels for electrons in an atom can also be explained by quanta.

⚙ During the 1920s, Erwin Schrödinger and Werner Heisenberg developed the idea of quantum energy levels in atoms to create a new branch of physics – called quantum physics.

▼ *The Large Hadron Collider at CERN, on the border between France and Switzerland, accelerates particles (such as protons) and smashes them together to create new particles that exist momentarily. This allows scientists to study the conditions of the early universe.*

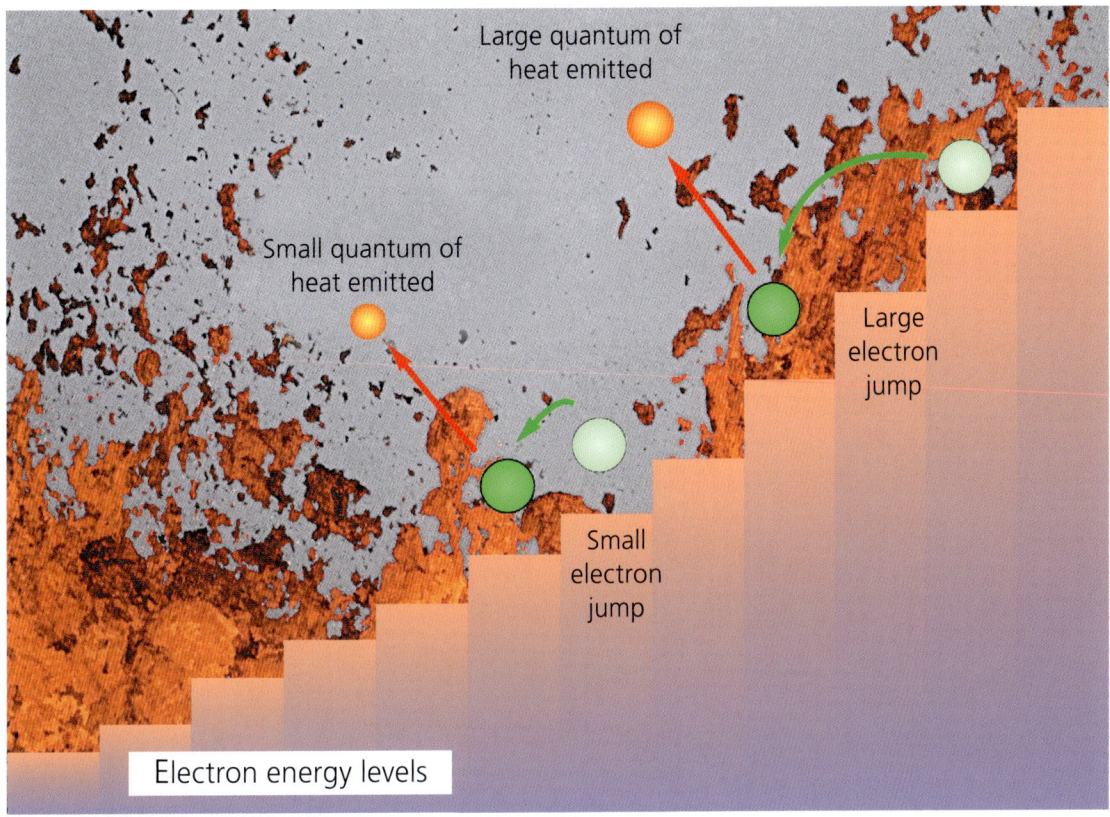

Large quantum of heat emitted

Small quantum of heat emitted

Large electron jump

Small electron jump

Electron energy levels

▲ *Quantum physics shows how radiation from a hot object is emitted in little chunks of energy named quanta.*

⚙ Quantum physics explains how electrons emit (give out) radiation (see pages 88–89). It demonstrates that an electron is both a particle and a wave, depending on the set-up of scientific experiments.

⚙ Quantum superposition is the theory that a quantum system can exist in multiple states at the same time – and only becomes fixed once it is measured by an observer.

⚙ This idea can be explored using the 'Schrödinger's cat' thought experiment, named after the physicist who suggested it – Erwin Schrödinger. The experiment asks you to imagine a cat trapped inside a sealed box with a bottle of poison. Until the box is opened, and an outsider observes the fate of the cat, the cat would theoretically exist as both alive and dead.

Nuclear energy

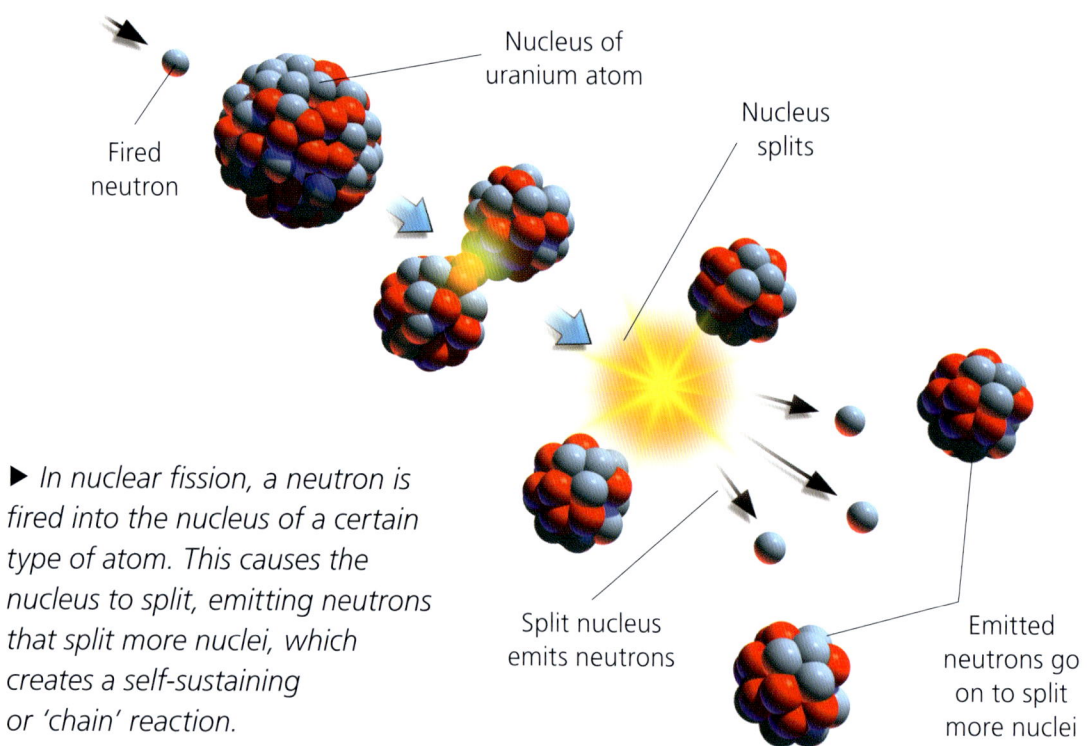

Nucleus of
uranium atom

Nucleus
splits

Fired
neutron

Split nucleus
emits neutrons

Emitted
neutrons go
on to split
more nuclei

▶ *In nuclear fission, a neutron is fired into the nucleus of a certain type of atom. This causes the nucleus to split, emitting neutrons that split more nuclei, which creates a self-sustaining or 'chain' reaction.*

⚙ The nucleus at the centre of each atom is bound together with lots and lots of energy. Releasing the energy from the nuclei of millions of atoms can generate a huge amount of power, known as nuclear power.

⚙ Any reaction that causes a change in the nucleus of an atom is known as a nuclear reaction.

⚙ Nuclear fission (above) is a process in which neutrons are fired at the large nuclei of atoms, such as uranium and plutonium, so that they split, releasing lots of energy.

⚙ As neutrons bombard (crash into) atoms and split their nuclei, the nuclei emit more neutrons. These neutrons bombard other nuclei, which emit more neutrons, and so on. This is called a chain reaction.

⚙ Nuclear fission is used in the generation of electricity (see page 116).

⚙ Nuclear fusion is the process in which small atoms such as deuterium (a form of hydrogen) are fused together to form a single, heavier nucleus, releasing huge amounts of energy in the process. The same process goes on in stars, such as our Sun, where hydrogen nuclei fuse together to build helium atoms.

⚙ An atom bomb (A-bomb) is one of the two main types of nuclear weapon. It works through an explosive, unrestrained fission of uranium-235 or plutonium-239.

⚙ A hydrogen bomb (H-bomb), or thermonuclear weapon, uses a conventional explosion to fuse the nuclei of deuterium atoms in a gigantic nuclear explosion.

▶ *The explosion of a nuclear weapon produces a characteristic 'mushroom cloud' that towers above the site of the explosion.*

Radioactivity

⚙️ Radioactivity is the spontaneous disintegration (breakdown) of a certain kind of atom. As it breaks up, the atom emits (sends out) little bursts of radiation.

⚙️ Isotopes are atoms of the same element that contain the same number of protons and electrons as each other (as in normal atoms) but different numbers of neutrons.

⚙️ A radioactive isotope is called a radioisotope. Some atoms, such as uranium, are so unstable that all of their isotopes are radioisotopes. These emit three types of radiation: alpha, beta and gamma rays.

New level of uranium-235

⚙️ When a large, unstable atomic nucleus disintegrates, it emits alpha and beta particles and becomes the atom of another element. This is known as radioactive decay.

New level of lead-207

⚙️ Alpha rays are streams of alpha particles. These are made up of two protons and two neutrons. Alpha rays can be stopped by a single sheet of paper.

⚙️ Beta rays are streams of beta particles – high-speed electrons (or positrons) that are emitted as a neutron decays into a proton. Beta particles are more penetrating, but a thin sheet of aluminium or a few millimetres of plastic can stop them.

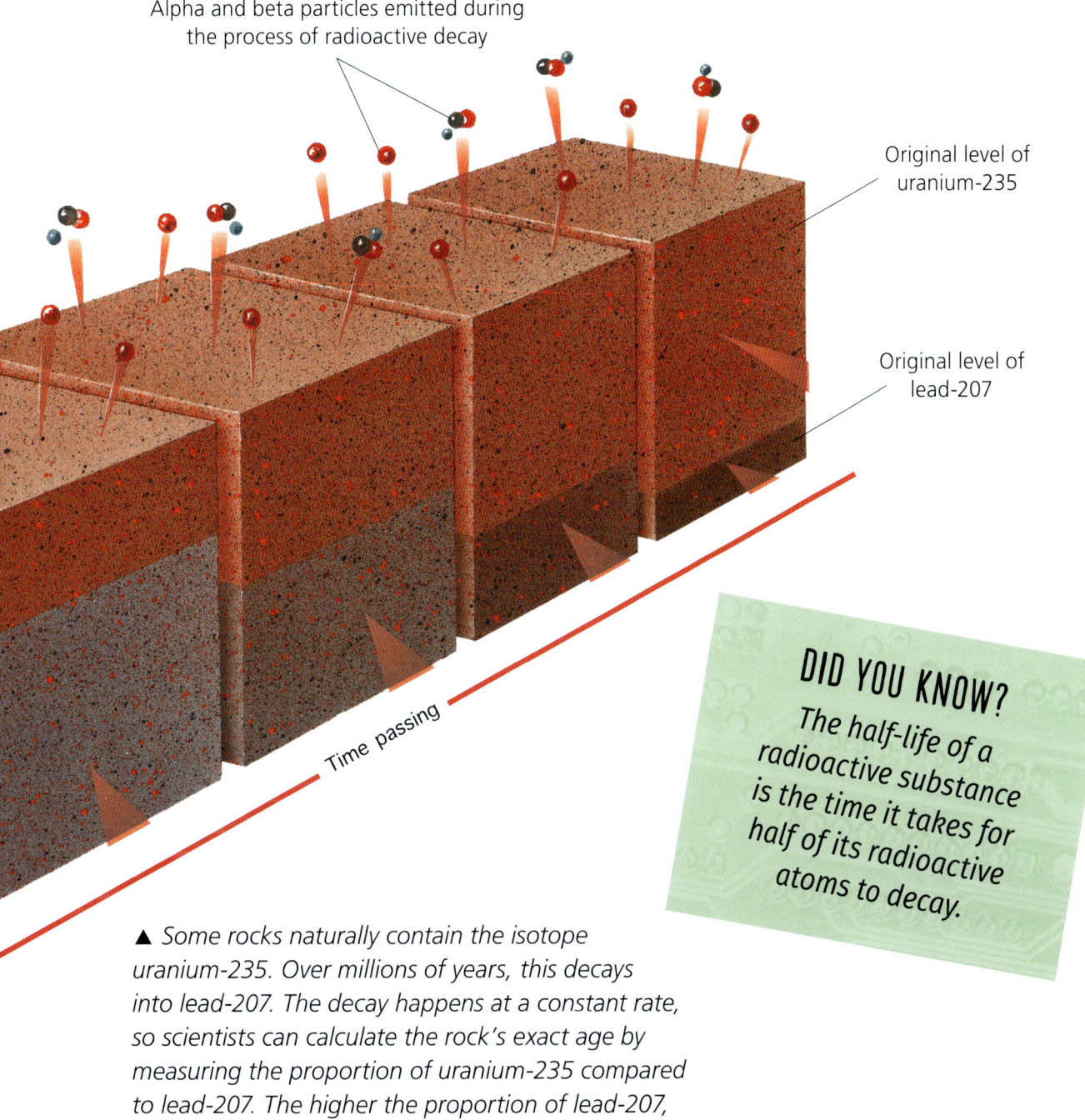

Alpha and beta particles emitted during
the process of radioactive decay

Original level of
uranium-235

Original level of
lead-207

Time passing

DID YOU KNOW?
The half-life of a
radioactive substance
is the time it takes for
half of its radioactive
atoms to decay.

▲ *Some rocks naturally contain the isotope
uranium-235. Over millions of years, this decays
into lead-207. The decay happens at a constant rate,
so scientists can calculate the rock's exact age by
measuring the proportion of uranium-235 compared
to lead-207. The higher the proportion of lead-207,
the older the rock.*

⚙ Gamma rays are electromagnetic waves of short wavelength and
high energy. They can penetrate most materials and are the most
dangerous form of radiation.

Splitting the atom

⚙ Atoms were thought to be solid and unbreakable until the 1890s.

⚙ In 1897, British physicist J J Thomson discovered that atoms contained even smaller particles, which he called electrons. He theorised that the electrons were studded into the surface of the atom. This model of the atom was called the 'plum pudding' model because of its resemblance to a Christmas pudding.

DID YOU KNOW?
The opposite of nuclear fission is nuclear fusion. This is when two small atoms are forced together to form a heavier atom.

⚙ Then, in 1909, New Zealand physicist Ernest Rutherford fired alpha particles at gold foil. Most went straight through the foil, but a few bounced back.

⚙ Rutherford concluded that atoms are mostly empty space (which the alpha particles passed through) but that each has a tiny, dense nucleus at its centre. Knowing that an atom is mostly empty space, this then raised the possibility that its nucleus could be split up.

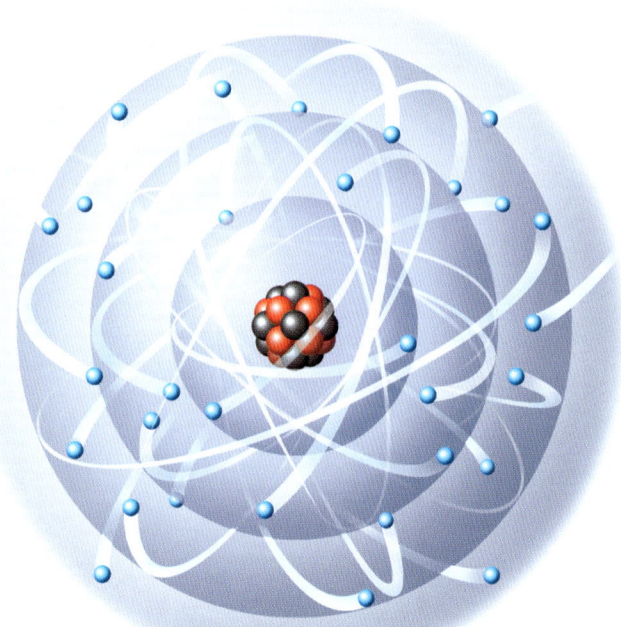

◀ The atom's nucleus, which makes up almost all of its mass, is made up of protons and neutrons. These are held together by a very strong force. By harnessing this force, nuclear energy is made.

▲ *It is not possible to see subatomic particles with our eyes – but after they collide, they leave tracks behind them that can be recorded photographically.*

⚙ In 1919, Rutherford split the nucleus of a nitrogen atom using alpha particles. Later, in 1932, James Chadwick showed that an atom's nucleus was made of two types of particle: neutrons and protons.

⚙ Beginning in 1934, Enrico Fermi and his team conducted an experiment that involved bombarding uranium atoms with 'slow neutrons'. At first, it appeared that the process might have created new chemical elements (with 93 and 94 protons), which his team called ausenium and hesperium. However, this was not quite true!

⚙ German scientists Otto Hahn and Fritz Strassmann repeated Fermi's experiment in 1938 – and found that the atoms created were, in fact, a radioactive form of a much lighter element called barium. This indicated that the uranium atom had split into two lighter atoms, a discovery that opened the way to releasing nuclear energy by fission.

Particle physics

▶ *Particle accelerators at Fermilab near Chicago (USA) and CERN (in France and Switzerland) accelerate particles to near light speed.*

New particles are fed in

Insulation inside tunnels prevents tiny particles from escaping

Massive detectors record collisions between particles

⚙ There are three basic, stable subatomic particles (electrons, protons and neutrons), but scientists have also found hundreds of other, 'unstable' types of particles. Most types of particles also have 'anti-particles', with the same mass but the opposite electrical charge.

⚙ Cosmic rays produce short-lived particles when they collide with air particles in the Earth's atmosphere. These include muons, a type of elementary particle. Muons are similar to electrons, but their mass is approximately 207 times greater.

⚙ Elementary particles are basic particles that cannot be broken down into anything smaller. There are three main groups of elementary particles: quarks, leptons and bosons.

⚙ Smashing atoms inside a particle accelerator creates short-lived, high-energy particles such as taus and pions – as well as heavier quarks, including 'charm', 'bottom' and 'top' quarks.

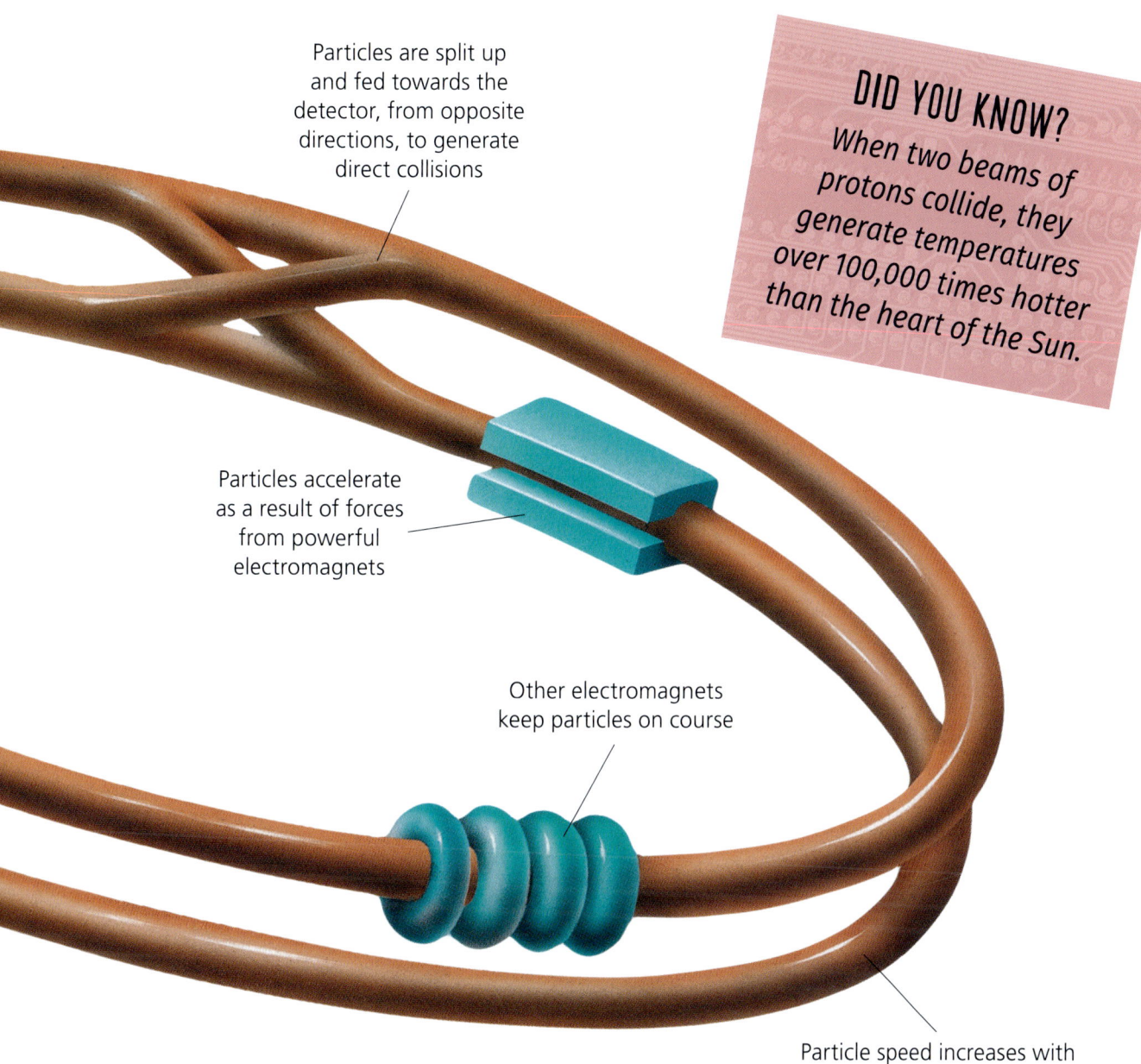

Particles are split up and fed towards the detector, from opposite directions, to generate direct collisions

DID YOU KNOW?
When two beams of protons collide, they generate temperatures over 100,000 times hotter than the heart of the Sun.

Particles accelerate as a result of forces from powerful electromagnets

Other electromagnets keep particles on course

Particle speed increases with each circuit of the tunnel

⚙ Particle accelerators are massive machines built inside tunnels. They use powerful magnets to accelerate particles through a tube (see above) at incredible speeds, and then smash them together.

⚙ Scientists classify particles using a framework called the Standard Model, in which they are divided into elementary particles and composite particles.

115

Nuclear power

⚙ Nuclear power harnesses the huge amount of energy that binds together the nucleus at the centre of atoms. It is an incredibly concentrated form of energy.

⚙ Nuclear energy is released through nuclear fission, in which the nuclei of atoms are split (see page 108).

⚙ Nuclear reactors do not burn fuel to produce their energy. Typically, their uranium fuel is processed into uranium dioxide ceramic pellets, which are then loaded into the reactor's fuel rods (see page 117).

⚙ A typical, 1,000-megawatt nuclear reactor uses approximately 27 tonnes of uranium fuel per year. The fresh, enriched uranium is processed into more than 18 million fuel pellets, which are then loaded into 50,000 or more fuel rods.

⚙ The earliest nuclear reactors were designed to make plutonium for use in nuclear weapons. Magnox reactors created plutonium, with electricity being generated as a by-product.

⚙ Like coal- and oil-fired power stations, nuclear power stations heat water to make steam. The steam is pressurised to drive the turbines that generate electricity. The main difference in a nuclear power station is that the immense heat comes from splitting uranium atoms (contained in the fuel) through a slow, controlled nuclear reaction.

⚙ Every stage of the nuclear process creates dangerous radioactive waste, which may take more than 10,000 years to become safe. Some mildly radioactive liquid waste is pumped out to sea. Gaseous waste is vented into the air. Any solid waste is mostly stockpiled underground.

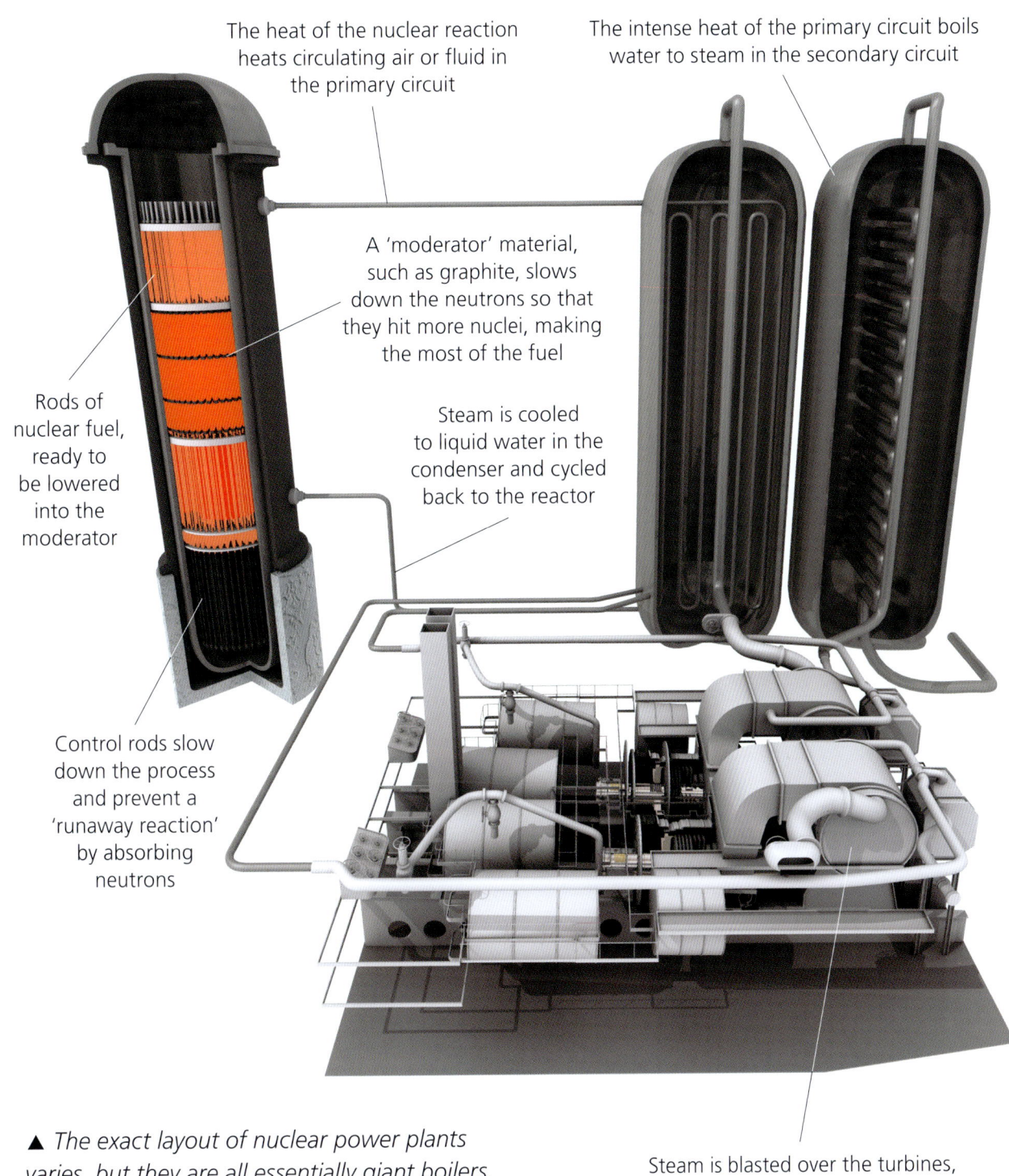

The heat of the nuclear reaction heats circulating air or fluid in the primary circuit

The intense heat of the primary circuit boils water to steam in the secondary circuit

A 'moderator' material, such as graphite, slows down the neutrons so that they hit more nuclei, making the most of the fuel

Rods of nuclear fuel, ready to be lowered into the moderator

Steam is cooled to liquid water in the condenser and cycled back to the reactor

Control rods slow down the process and prevent a 'runaway reaction' by absorbing neutrons

Steam is blasted over the turbines, which are connected to generators that produce electricity

▲ *The exact layout of nuclear power plants varies, but they are all essentially giant boilers, designed to use nuclear reactions to heat water, which creates high-pressure steam to drive the spinning turbines that generate electricity.*

Genetic engineering

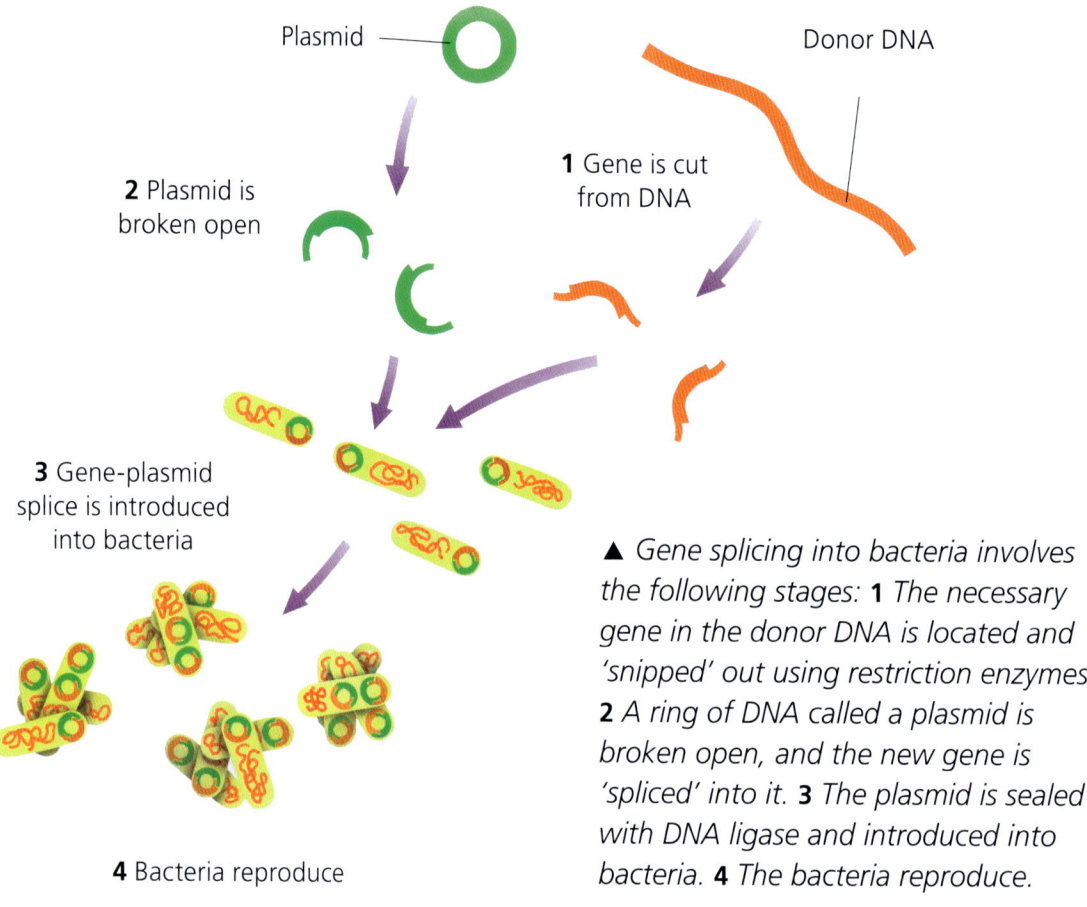

Plasmid

Donor DNA

2 Plasmid is broken open

1 Gene is cut from DNA

3 Gene-plasmid splice is introduced into bacteria

4 Bacteria reproduce

▲ *Gene splicing into bacteria involves the following stages:* **1** *The necessary gene in the donor DNA is located and 'snipped' out using restriction enzymes.* **2** *A ring of DNA called a plasmid is broken open, and the new gene is 'spliced' into it.* **3** *The plasmid is sealed with DNA ligase and introduced into bacteria.* **4** *The bacteria reproduce.*

⚙ Genetics is the science of heredity, dealing with how organisms pass on traits (or characteristics) to their offspring, or young.

⚙ A gene is the basic unit of inheritance that tells an organism how to grow and live. It comes as a short section of chemical code on special molecules, present in every living cell, called DNA.

⚙ Genetic engineering involves deliberately manipulating the genes of organisms to give them specific characteristics.

⚙ Scientists alter genes by snipping them from the DNA of one organism and inserting them into the DNA of another. This is known as gene splicing. The altered DNA is called recombinant DNA.

⚙ Genes are cut from DNA using 'biological scissors' called restriction enzymes. They are spliced into DNA using 'biological glue' known as DNA ligase.

⚙ Once a cell has altered DNA, every new cell it produces will also have the altered DNA.

⚙ Genetically modified (GM) food is produced from animals or plants that have had their genes altered. For example, a food crop can be genetically modified to make it resistant to pests or frost.

⚙ Gene therapy is an experimental science in which human genes are altered in order to cure diseases that have been inherited from parents, or caused by faulty genes.

⚙ Cloning means creating an organism with exactly the same genes as another. In nature, organisms contain a mixture of genes from two parents. Cloning takes DNA from a single donor and uses it to 'grow' a new life. The new life has exactly the same genes as the donor of the DNA. Full DNA cloning of an entire individual has been achieved in plants and animals – but not in human beings.

⚙ In 2020, chemists Jennifer Doudna and Emmanuelle Charpentier were awarded the Nobel prize in Chemistry for their development of the CRISPR-Cas9 gene editing technology – also known as 'genetic scissors'.

▶ *Genetic engineers have created mice that glow green by giving them a specific gene (taken from a species of jellyfish) known as Green Fluorescent Protein (or GFP).*

Electric power

⚙ Electric power is provided by moving electrons, tiny bursts of energy that can travel through metals and other conductors. The electricity we use in our homes comes from huge power stations and is carried around the country through a network of cables.

⚙ In most power stations, a generator produces electricity by turning a wire coil within a magnetic field – for example, between two large magnets. The coil is connected by an axle (a rotating shaft) to a turbine, which is like a fan with many blades. As the turbine spins, it rotates the coil to 'shift' the electrons and induce (produce) an electric current. This process is called electromagnetic induction.

⚙ Traditional power stations burn coal or oil to boil water, producing high-pressure steam that drives the turbine, or burn gas to drive it directly. As burning fossil fuels contributes to climate change, many countries are adopting cleaner, renewable sources of electricity.

⚙ The turbine of a hydroelectric power station is driven by the controlled flow of water through a dam.

⚙ A nuclear power station uses the radioactive decay of plutonium or uranium to heat water and drive a turbine (see pages116–117).

⚙ Wind turbines (right) use the wind's natural kinetic energy to turn aerodynamic blades, which spin a rotor. The spinning of the rotor drives an electrical generator, housed inside the 'nacelle' at the top of each tower.

⚙ Solar panels generate electricity directly from sunlight, without the need for a turbine. Photons in sunlight knock electrons out of a semi-conductive material, such as silicon, creating a flow of electricity.

DID YOU KNOW?
The world's biggest solar power station is Golmud Solar Park, in China. It has more than 7 million solar panels, generating around 2,800 megawatts of power.

▲ *A group of wind turbines is called a wind farm. Each of these large turbines is about 90–100 m tall, with blades of around 65 m in length. Given the right conditions, one large wind turbine can produce around 6 million kilowatt hours (kWh) of electricity every year – enough to power approximately 1,500 homes.*

⚙ Electricity from power stations is distributed around a country in a network of cables known as 'the grid'. Tall structures, called pylons, carry the cables across large expanses of land or countryside.

⚙ Power station generators produce around 25,000 volts of electricity. To transmit it over long distances, the voltage is boosted to 400,000 volts by transformers. It can then be transmitted through high-voltage cables. Near its destination, the voltage is reduced – at electricity substations – to a level safe for use in homes and businesses.

Computers

⚙ Computers are essentially thinking machines. They process data (information you feed into them) following a set of instructions known as programmes, or software.

⚙ The information, or data, that a computer requires to work is stored in microchips – tiny structures of electronic components and their connections, etched onto tiny slices of silicon (see page 85).

⚙ Computers use both hardware and software to function. Hardware refers to the physical parts of the computer, whereas software refers to things like code, programmes and applications.

⚙ All the data you put into a computer – including words, pictures and videos – are converted to positive and negative electric charges, or 'on' and 'off' states, represented by a sequence of 1s and 0s. This is called binary code. The computer uses binary code for storing and processing data, whether you are writing an essay, storing digital photos or recording a video.

⚙ A single digit of binary code is known as a bit. Eight bits make a byte. Approximately one million bytes is a megabyte (MB), one billion bytes is a gigabyte (GB) and roughly one trillion bytes is a terabyte (TB).

⚙ Computers were originally the size of a room and a lot less powerful than a modern smartphone. Today, we have dedicated personal computers, laptops and tablets. Many other machines and appliances (including washing machines, fridges and microwaves) use computer technology, such as microcontrollers, to perform their functions.

⚙ Smartphones and smartwatches are computers. They use microchips and software to let you stream videos and use apps. A smart TV can connect you to streaming services, store programmes for you to watch later and suggest content based on what you've watched before.

⚙ Equipment with 'smart' technology uses tiny computers to store information about your preferences and choices. It also allows you to control the equipment remotely from a phone or laptop.

⚙ A smart car can be set to find a route to your destination, or to park by itself. It uses sensors to detect obstacles, and connects to the Internet to retrieve maps and information about road conditions.

⚙ A smart fridge can track the kind of foods you use, and has cameras that enable you to check inside it from a smartphone, while shopping, to see what you have and what you might need to buy.

▼ *Programmers use computing languages such as JavaScript or Python to design and create computer code. This code acts as a series of instructions that tell the computer what to do. All computer software is composed of computer code.*

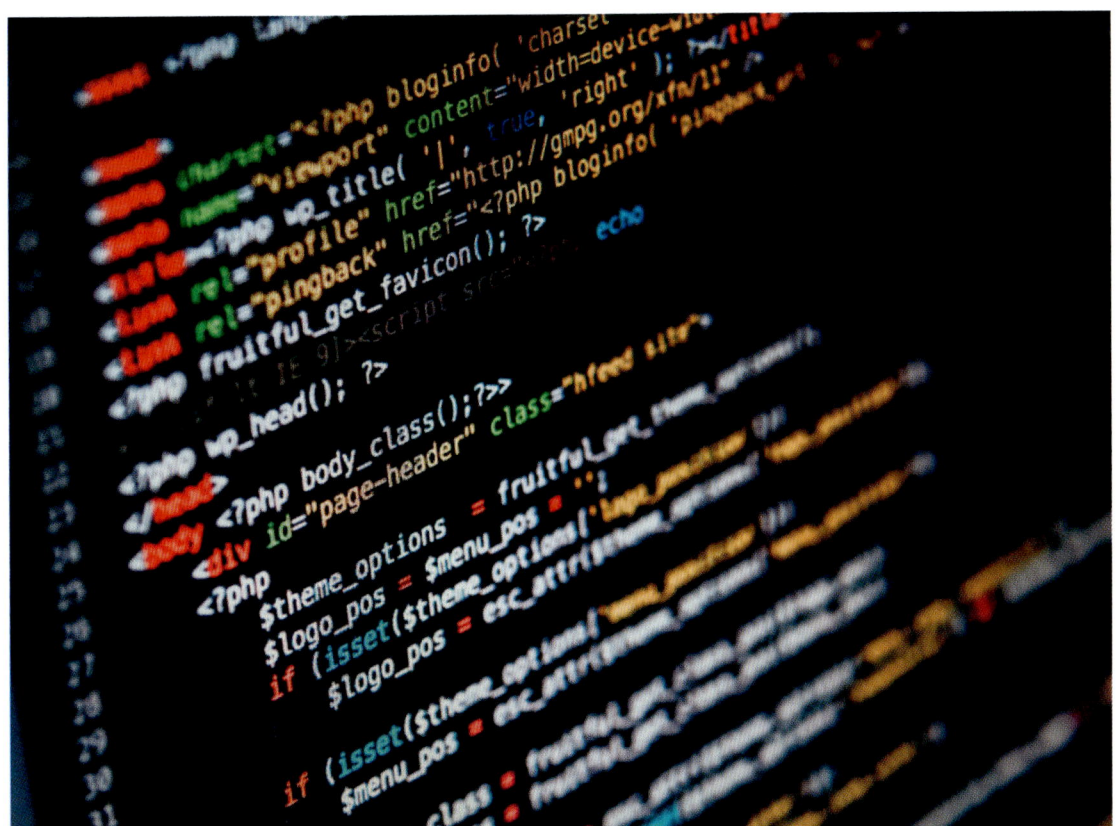

123

Robotics

⚙ Robots are machines that can be programmed to carry out specific tasks or functions without any human help. Some also use artificial intelligence (AI) to 'learn' from past results and improve their performance over time.

⚙ The first programmable robot was an industrial robot called Unimate, made in the 1950s. It had an arm that could pick things up.

⚙ Robots work quickly and tirelessly and can do repetitive work without getting bored or exhausted. They have been used in factories since the early 1960s. Custom-made robots have been developed to build tiny, delicate components that are too small for people to handle easily, and to lift and place heavy objects safely and precisely.

⚙ Sensors that detect conditions such as light, movement, sound or heat enable robots to 'see' or 'hear'. This means that they can respond to their environment and work out the right thing to do next.

⚙ Robots can work in places that are too dangerous for people to work in. They have been used to explore under the sea, around active volcanoes, and even in space.

⚙ The Mars rover *Perseverance* combines data it gathers using its sensors with its programming to 'decide' which Martian rocks are worth investigating. It then collects, grinds and examines the rocks.

⚙ Some robots work independently, while others are directed by people. Surgical robots are controlled by an expert surgeon. They carry out the detailed and careful work of surgery with a steadier hand and sharper eye than even the best human surgeons!

DID YOU KNOW?
The term 'robotics' was first used by science fiction writer Isaac Asimov. He also developed the three 'Laws of Robotics', guidelines for how robots should behave.

▲ *Robotic animals, such as this high-tech dog, use cameras, sensors and LiDAR (Light Detection and Ranging) technology to build up a 3D map of the environment around them. They use this information to navigate and avoid obstacles.*

⚙ Scientists are developing microscopic robots, or nanobots, that might one day be used to perform surgery from inside a person's body.

⚙ There are robots all around us, from aerial drones taking pictures from the sky to self-driving cars and autonomous vacuum cleaners that whizz around the floor, cleaning up dust and dirt by themselves.

125

Seeing the microworld

⚙ Microscopes are devices used for looking at and examining things that are normally too small for the human eye to see.

⚙ An optical microscope uses 'convex' lenses to converge or bend light rays together at a focal point, magnifying what you see through the viewfinder (see below). Today's advanced optical microscopes can make a single molecule visible.

⚙ Scanning Electron Microscopes (SEMs) use a focused beam of electrons that scan the surface of an object, causing various signals to be emitted. A computer processes the information to create a sharp image of the sample object on a screen.

⚙ SEMs can magnify an object up to a million or even two million times. Some SEMs can even focus on an object that is 1 nanometre (one-billionth of a metre) across and magnify it five million times. They are so powerful that they can make individual atoms visible.

◄ *Microscopes are essential for laboratory work that involves examining very small samples, such as bacteria, viruses and human body cells.*

⚙ A Transmission Electron Microscope (TEM) shines electrons through very thin slices of an object, which are then focused and magnified to make the specimen around a million times bigger.

⚙ Powerful TEMs, such as the TEAM 0.5 microscope, can make objects smaller than a hydrogen atom (the smallest of all atoms) visible.

⚙ Scanning Acoustic Microscopy (SAM) uses sound waves to see inside tiny, opaque objects (those that block the passage of radiant energy, such as light).

▼ *Scientists can use electron microcopes to view the structure of body cells. This TEM image of a nerve cell (right) has been coloured to show its different components, such as the nucleus (purple).*

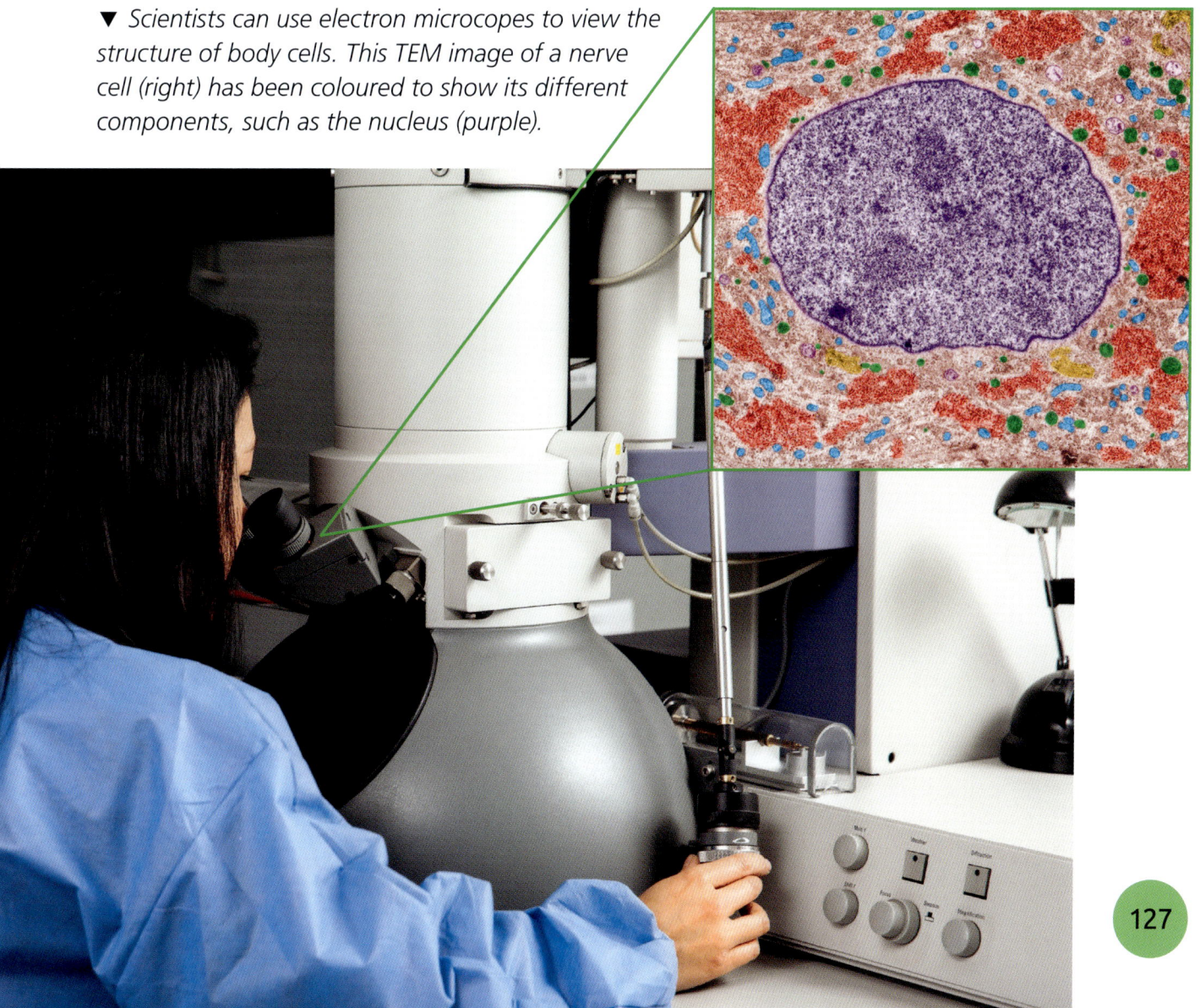

Light fibres

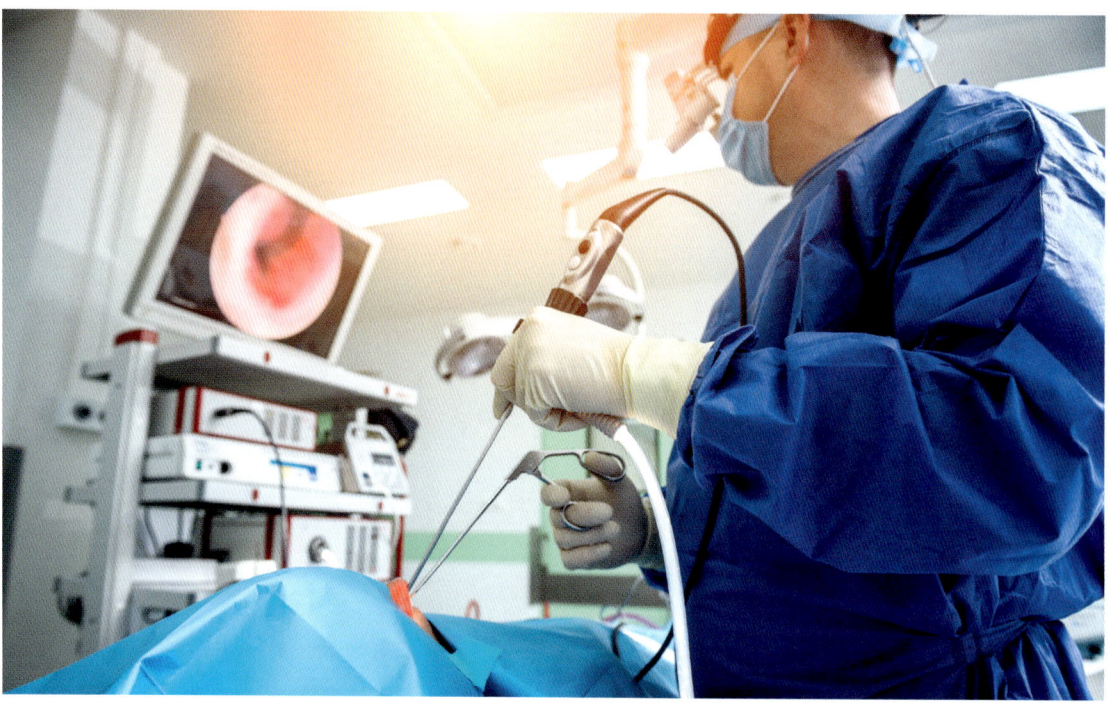

▲ *An endoscope is a tube that can be inserted into the body to view internal organs. Images from inside the body are sent along flexible optical fibres to a viewing screen.*

⚙ Optical fibres are threads of transparent glass. Bundles of these threads are known as fibre-optic cables, and are used to transmit data and messages as light signals.

⚙ For data to be transmitted using fibre-optics, it must be turned into a digital form – a series of binary 'on/off' signals made up of 1s and 0s (see page 122).

⚙ These signals power a light source at the end of a fibre to pulse 'on' and 'off'. This signal then travels along optical fibres until it reaches its destination, where circuits turn it back into an electrical signal.

⚙ The largest fibre-optic cables can carry hundreds of thousands of phone calls or hundreds of television channels.

⚙ There are fibre-optic cables laid across the world's oceans.

Lasers

⚙ A laser is a device that creates a bright artificial light. A beam of laser light is so intense that it can cut through tough materials such as steel. In relation to their size, some lasers are brighter than the Sun.

⚙ The word 'laser' is an acronym for Light Amplification by Stimulated Emission of Radiation.

⚙ Laser light is the only known 'coherent' source of light. Coherent means that its light waves are all of the same frequency (wavelength) and all the same phase (the peaks and troughs of the waves all align).

⚙ Inside a laser is a small space filled with a 'lasing' material – either a gas (such as neon or xenon) or a liquid or solid crystal (such as ruby).

⚙ A burst of photons (particles of electromagnetic radiation) excites atoms in the lasing material. The excited atoms emit photons. When the photons hit other atoms, they fire off photons, too, which bounce to and fro off of mirrors inside the space. This amplifies the light.

⚙ The powerful laser beam finally exits the space through a small hole.

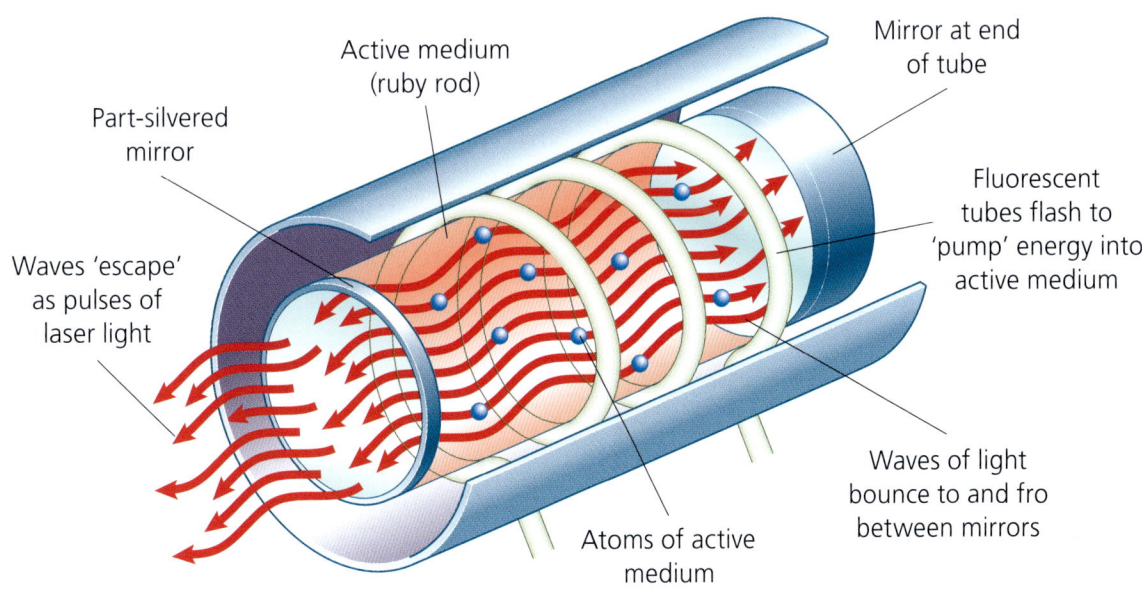

Active medium (ruby rod)

Mirror at end of tube

Part-silvered mirror

Fluorescent tubes flash to 'pump' energy into active medium

Waves 'escape' as pulses of laser light

Waves of light bounce to and fro between mirrors

Atoms of active medium

▲ In a ruby laser, energy is put into a ruby rod – the 'active medium' – as high-energy pulses of ordinary light.

129

Television

⚙ Modern television (TV) screens build up pictures using individual pixels, the tiny dots that make up an image. Pixel-based display technologies, such as LED or OLED, create the colour images by instructing individual pixels to either emit (release) or block light.

⚙ Nearly all of today's TV cameras are digital. Light information is focused by a lens, in the usual way, then light-sensitive, electronic image sensors, such as CMOS sensors, convert the light into digital signals, ready to be displayed as images. The digital images can either be stored or transmitted in real time as a 'live' broadcast.

▲ *You can watch television in a variety of ways. Broadcast TV follows a set programme schedule that you can access via television channels, whereas 'streaming' allows viewers to watch shows or movies provided by an online service – using devices such as PCs, tablets and smartphones. This live broadcast of a news conference (above) can be streamed directly via the internet – a process also known as webcasting.*

DID YOU KNOW?
The first purely electronic television systems, with no moving parts, were developed in the 1920s and '30s.

⚙ Older, non-digital TV broadcasting, known as analogue, used the varying strength of radio signals to carry information for pictures and sound.

⚙ Digital broadcasting carries information in the form of millions of binary 'on/off' signals (coded as 1s and 0s) every second.

⚙ Most current TV sets have flat screens that use LED (Light-Emitting Diode) or LCD (Liquid Crystal Display) technologies. These have steadily taken over from the older, heavier, box-like glass-screen displays known as CRTs (or cathode-ray tubes).

⚙ A 'plasma screen' has millions of tiny compartments, or cells, and two sets of wire-like electrodes at right angles to each other. Each cell can be 'addressed' by sending electrical pulses along two electrodes that cross that cell.

⚙ These electrical pulses heat the cell's gas into plasma, making a coloured substance (phosphor) glow. The overall picture we see is built up by millions of pulses taking place – every second – at different 'addresses' all over the screen.

⚙ Programme providers broadcast TV shows on set frequencies known as television channels. The schedule of programmes to be broadcast is often organised weeks or months in advance.

⚙ Live TV is any televised programme that is broadcast in real time as the events take place.

⚙ Streaming television is television that is being viewed 'on demand' through an internet connection. This allows viewers to watch what they want, when they want. You can access streaming TV through a smart TV, personal computer, smartphone, tablet or gaming console.

Digital recording

⚙ Digital recording is a process in which sounds or pictures are recorded as a series of binary digits (1s and 0s).

⚙ Before digital processes came along, sound and picture recordings were analogue – where the signals are recorded continuously as matching physical changes on a tape or a disc. When the sound is loud, for instance, the changes are larger.

⚙ Analogue recordings add 'noise' (or interference) during the recording process. If a quiet recording is amplified (increased in strength), the added noise is also amplified.

⚙ With digital systems, there is no noise added during reproduction or amplification. This is because the recorder simply sends only the digital code of the recording to the player, which might be a TV, a computer or a music system. The player recreates the original sound from the digital code 'cleanly', with little or no interference.

▼ *External drives are one of the many ways in which people store their data digitally. Hard drive discs permanently store information on magnetically coated, spinning 'hard' discs. More modern, Solid-State Drives or SSDs (below) permanently store information on flash-memory chips, making them less fragile.*

▲ *Using photo-editing software, computers can make changes to digital images. For example, the computer can be instructed to make an image appear brighter, change the hue, or even add or remove objects.*

⚙ Digital radio and TV broadcasts can be very clear, because the digital code is always the same – no matter how strong or faint the signal might be.

⚙ Digital imaging allows faint sounds and pictures to be amplified without any interference or distortion.

⚙ It is possible to process digital images on a computer to accentuate (emphasize) certain features or qualities – and play down others.

⚙ Astronomers have used digital imaging techniques to identify very distant, faint stars and galaxies.

⚙ Mathematically 'compressing' the digits in a digital recording allows very detailed, 'high resolution' recordings to be made and transmitted, including mp3 sound recordings and High Definition (HD) TV pictures.

Scanning

⚙ A scanner is an electronic device that traces out and builds up an image in lines.

⚙ Image scanners convert pictures or text into a digital form that computers can read.

⚙ A photoelectric cell inside the scanner measures the amount of light reflected from each part of the object, or document, and converts this into a binary digital code (of 1s and 0s).

⚙ Complex scanning devices are used in medicine to produce pictures of internal organs or body parts. These include CT scanners, PET scanners and MRI scanners.

▼ *Unlike X-rays, an MRI scanner does not produce potentially harmful radiation.*

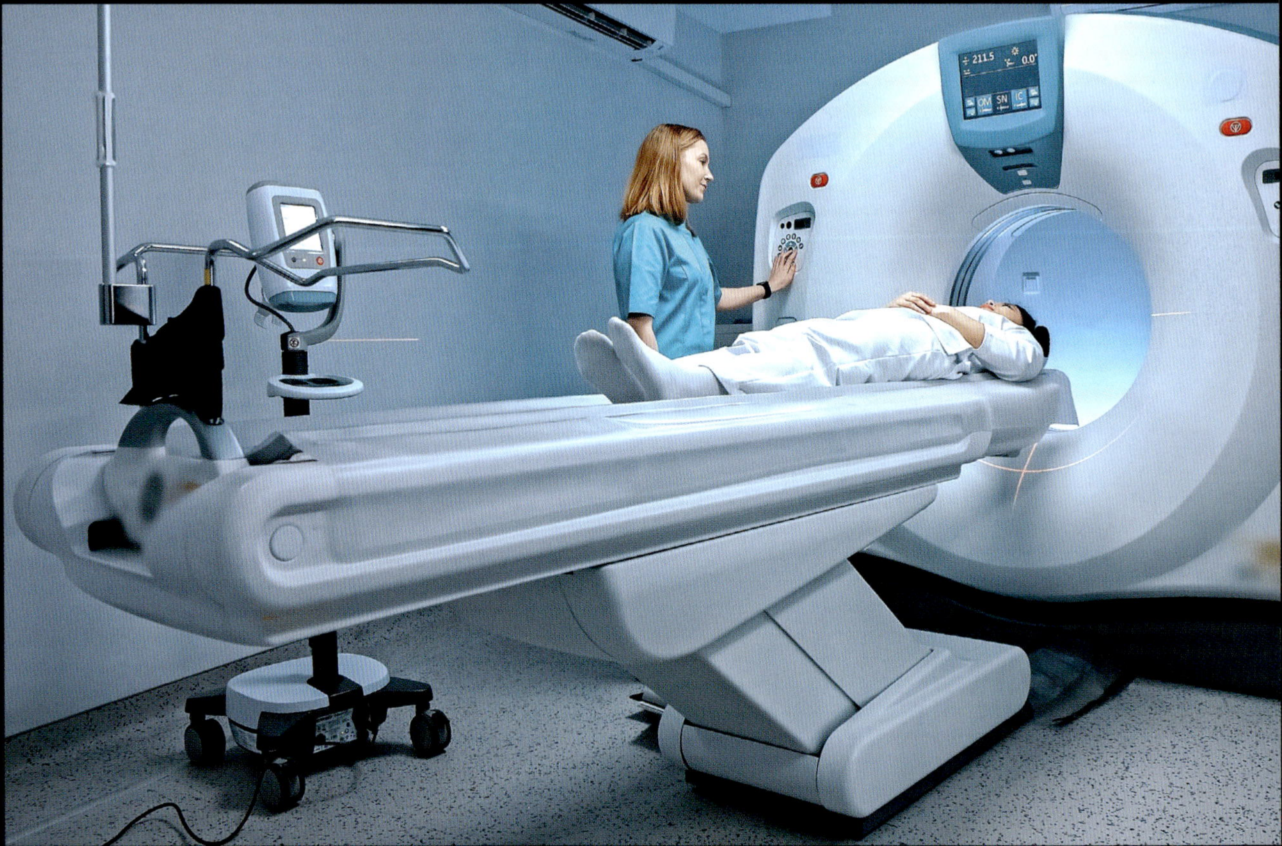

⚙ CT stands for Computed Tomography. In CT scanning, an X-ray beam rotates around the patient and is picked up by detectors on the far side to build up a detailed, 3D image of the inside of the patient's body.

⚙ PET stands for Positron Emission Tomography. In PET scanning, the scanner picks up positrons (positively charged electrons) sent out by substances injected into the blood. PET scans can literally 'visualise' the activity of a living brain.

⚙ MRI stands for Magnetic Resonance Imaging. MRI scans work in a similar way to CT scans, but use magnetism instead of X-rays. In an MRI, the patient is surrounded by magnets, which cause all the protons in the body to line up.

⚙ An MRI scan starts as a radio pulse that knocks protons briefly out of alignment. The scanner then detects radio signals sent out by the protons as they snap back into line. These signals are translated by a computer into detailed images.

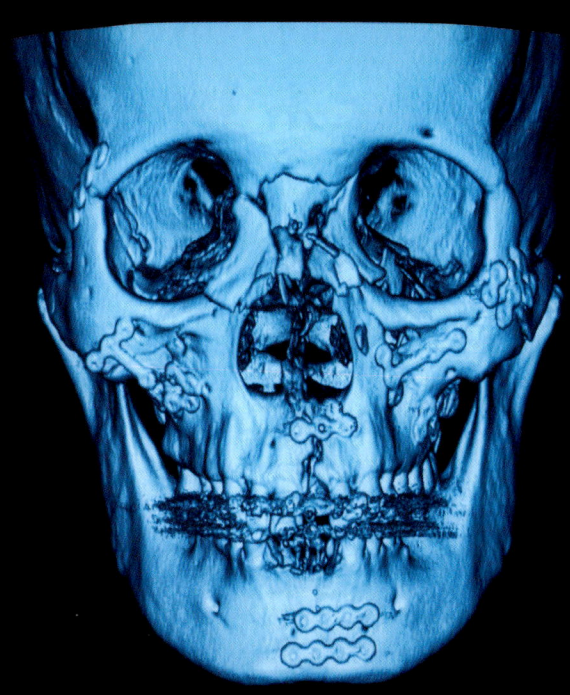

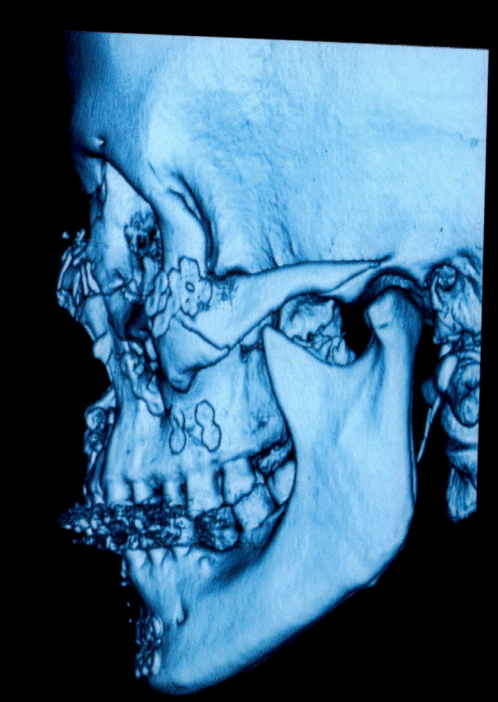

▲ *In these CT scans of a human skull and facial bones, the picture is built up and the colours are*

Internet

⚙ The Internet is a worldwide network of computers linked by cables, and wirelessly by radio, used to store and share data and information of many types. It began as a small network of university computers in the USA in the 1960s.

⚙ Use of the Internet by the general population increased massively after the invention of the World Wide Web in 1989, by English computer programmer Tim Berners-Lee. 1991 saw the public launch of his first-ever web page.

⚙ These days, we use the Internet for almost all our communications, from email to video calls, radio and television transmissions.

⚙ Many people use the Internet to read the news, keep in touch with friends and interest groups through social media, and to access streaming sites for entertainment. The Internet provides near-instantaneous communication.

⚙ Online gaming allows people to play fast video games with other players scattered around the world, all connected over the Internet.

⚙ Most business is now conducted over the internet, using transactions such as online ordering, shopping, banking and money transfers.

▶ *Online gamers often use headsets with microphones, so that they can record a commentary for gaming videos and streams, or communicate with their fellow players in real time.*

⚙ More and more devices are connected to the Internet every year, including 'smart' devices and appliances in homes, such as fridges and TVs, and wearable devices including watches and fitness trackers. These gadgets collect data and track patterns of use, and allow users to access their devices remotely.

⚙ There is a dark side to the Internet, too. It has made new types of crime possible, such as cyber fraud, identity theft, and threatening or abusing people online. The Internet has also been used to spread disinformation (information intended to mislead people) and hate.

⚙ Cybersecurity and programming are growing global industries.

▲ *Social media websites and apps are interactive media where most of the content is created by the users. Different forms of social media have been designed to host different types of content, and to cater for different personal or professional interests.*

Telecommunications

⚙ Telecommunications involve different types of data being transmitted, over various distances, by electronic processes.

⚙ Every communication system requires three things to function: a transmitter, a communications channel (or medium) and a receiver.

⚙ Transmitters convert data (text, images or sounds) into an electrical signal and send it. Transmitters include radio stations, mobile phones, computers and Bluetooth devices.

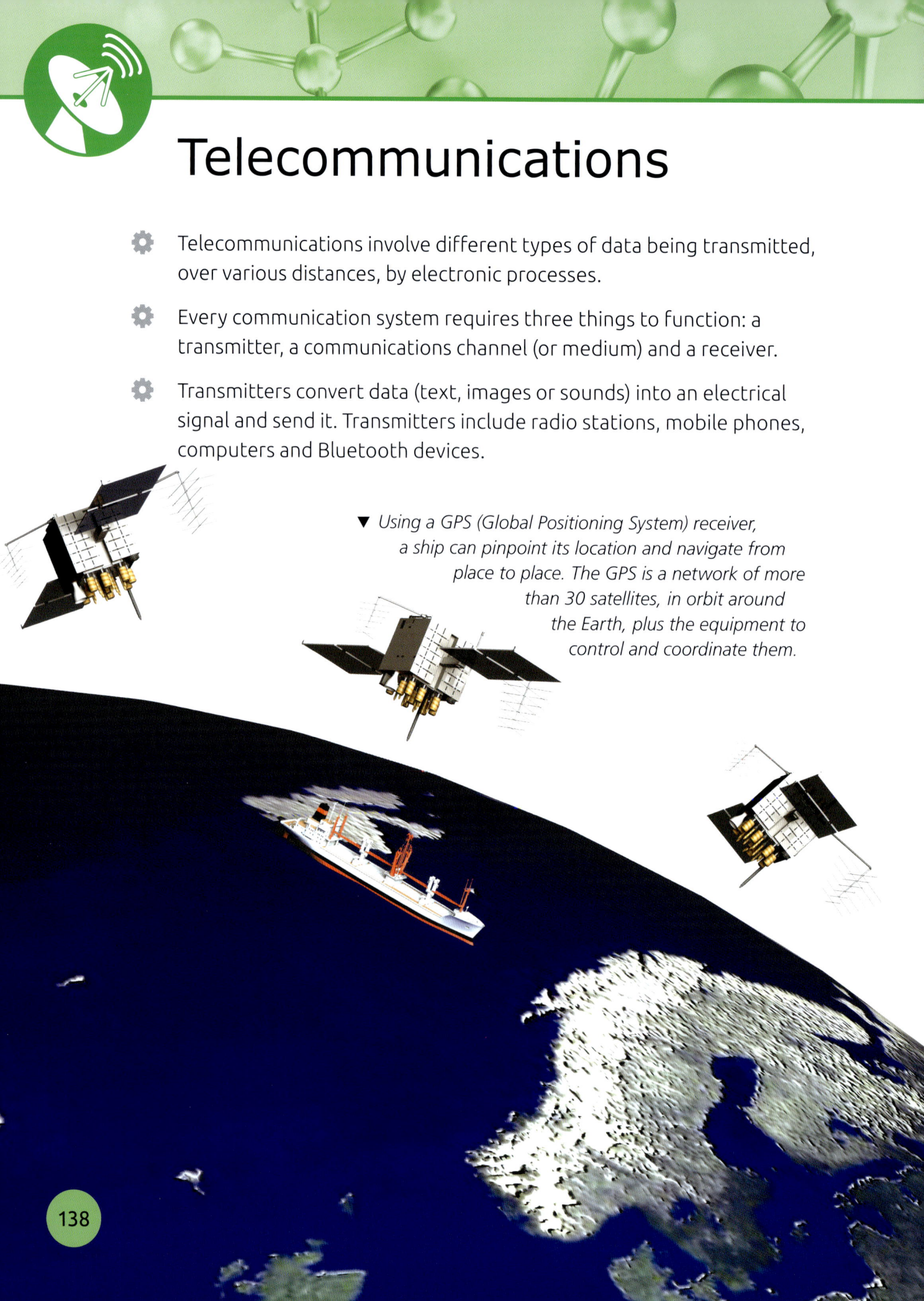

▼ *Using a GPS (Global Positioning System) receiver, a ship can pinpoint its location and navigate from place to place. The GPS is a network of more than 30 satellites, in orbit around the Earth, plus the equipment to control and coordinate them.*

⚙ Receivers pick up the electrical signal and convert it back into its original form.

⚙ Communications links, or channels, carry the signal from the transmitter to the receiver in two main ways: some give a direct link through telephone lines and other cables, while others are carried on radio waves through the air, via satellite or microwave links, or via mobile phone towers.

⚙ In the past, telephone lines have mainly been composed of electrical cables, which carried the signal as pulses of electricity. Today, telephone lines are usually fibre-optic cables, which carry the signals as coded pulses of light.

⚙ Communications satellites are machines in space, orbiting the Earth. Telephone calls are beamed up on radio waves to a satellite, which then beams them back down to another part of the world.

⚙ Microwave links use very short radio waves to transmit telephone and other signals directly from one dish to another – in a straight, 'line-of-sight' path – across the Earth's surface.

⚙ Mobile or cellular phones transmit and receive phone calls directly via radio waves. Calls are picked up and sent on from a local aerial mast (or base station), which routes the call through the network to the correct recipient.

⚙ The Internet is not totally wireless! The content and data that reaches our homes and businesses relies on a vast, physical network of connected systems, including Internet Service Providers (ISPs), fibre-optic cables, routers and data centres.

Index

Page numbers in **bold** refer to main entries; page numbers in *italics* refer to illustrations.